MONTREAL
A BRIEF
HISTORY

JOHN IRWIN COOPER

MONTREAL AND LONDON
McGILL-QUEEN'S UNIVERSITY PRESS
1969

© John Irwin Cooper 1969
Type set in the United Kingdom
by H. G. Walters Ltd.
Printed in Canada
by John Deyell Limited
Designed by Einar Vinje
Library of Congress Catalog Card No. 72-96842
SBN 7735-0053-7

PREFACE

This history of Montreal is weighted towards modern times: the half-century before Confederation and the full century since. The century and three quarters before that time—over half of Montreal's lifetime—is dealt with in summary form only.

I am writing in outline, in order to set out the main course clearly and strongly. Secondary themes are omitted, fascinating though some of them may be. Details are used only to give depth. Even in introducing the names of individuals, the same selectivity has been exercised, and many who made worthwhile contributions to Montreal have had to go unmentioned.

I wish to present Montreal's people in action and to show the forces that brought about change. In earning their living, Montrealers have done a variety of jobs. Three hundred, even two hundred, years ago, they were fur takers and furtraders. One hundred years ago, they were engaged chiefly in general commerce. Today, they follow a bewildering variety of occupations.

In meeting the changing world around them, they encountered problems that were common to other growing cities. Problems and conditions that were peculiar to Montreal came from the character and institutions of French Canada: Quebec has its own civil code, based on the Code Napoléon, while the rest of Canada uses English common law. In Quebec, the Roman Catholic Church is *the* Church in a sense that no other church is anywhere else in North America.

As Montreal grew and served Canada, so Canada built Montreal. The city's history belongs to all Canadians, not just to Montrealers. Perhaps other cities will use Montreal's history as a dateline along which they can check off their own starting points and progress. They may have begun with the fur trade, or with the coming of the railway; with the introduction of electricity, or with the automobile.

Anyone who wishes to flesh out the skeleton here presented would do well to read Hector Berthelot's *Montréal, le bon vieux temps* (Montréal: Beauchemin, 1916), 'compilé, revu et annoté par E. - Z. Massicotte', E. A. Collard's *Montreal Yesterdays* and *Call Back Yesterdays* (Toronto: Longmans, 1962 and 1965), Olivier Maurault's *Marges d'histoire* (3 vols.; Montréal: Librairie d'Action canadienne-française, 1929-30), and T. P. Slattery's *Loyola and Montreal* (Montreal: Palm Publishers, 1962), where justice is done to Montreal's humour, vivacity, and charm.

It is a pleasure to acknowledge the generous help I have received. My thanks are due to McGill University and to the Canada Council for making it possible for me to put in book form a continuing interest of many years. I also wish to thank Dr. D. G. G. Kerr of the University of Western Ontario for his encouragement and critical guidance.

I have drawn heavily on archives and libraries. My debt to them began long before the writing of the current history. I wish to acknowledge the assistance I have received from the Archives of the City of Montreal; the Archives de la Province de Québec; the Public Archives of Canada; the Château de Ramézay; the Archives of the Canadian National and Canadian Pacific railways, Molson's Brewery, the Montreal Board of Trade, and the Montreal Transportation Commission; the libraries of the cities of Montreal and Westmount, the Ecole des Hautes Etudes commerciales, McGill University and the Université de Montréal; the Bibliothèque de Saint-Sulpice; the Fraser-Hickson Institute; the Library of Parliament. I wish to thank the officers of a number of corporations: The British Petroleum Corporation; Dupuis Frères; The T. Eaton Company; Holt Renfrew and Company; The Imperial Oil Company of Canada; the Henry Morgan Company; Texaco Canada Limited.

To Mary Delight Cooper for her criticism and countless hours of devoted labour in revision and final writing, I can give no adequate form of recognition.

CONTENTS

1 EARLY MONTREAL 1642-1817

At the time of Confederation in 1867, Montreal was two centuries and a quarter old. It ranked, therefore, as one of the older North American cities, certainly of those north of the Rio Grande. In Canada, only Quebec was Montreal's senior; in the United States, only St. Augustine, New York, and Boston. The achievement of Montreal since Confederation has been based solidly on what was accomplished before Confederation. In summary, what may be said of the first two hundred and twenty-five years?[1]

DISCOVERY AND THE FRENCH FACT

The Island of Montreal was discovered and settled by French people. These are basic facts in any consideration of its history. The first European to reach the site of Montreal was the Breton seaman, Jacques Cartier. His coming in October 1535 established the primacy of French interests. About seventy years later (1603), Samuel de Champlain, the agent of French trading and colonizing enterprises, visited the Island. Between that date and his death in 1635, Champlain was there on a number of occasions. The most important was in 1611, when he fully explored the neighbourhood. Champlain, who was a geographer, was able to appreciate the Island's many advantages: about thirty miles in length and ten in width, it was the largest of a group of islands lying at the junction of the St. Lawrence and Ottawa rivers; it was a thousand miles inland from the sea, at the breaking-point of ocean and river navigation. Champlain's explorations and writings permanently fixed French interests in Montreal and led directly to the first French settlement in 1642.[2]

To Cartier and Champlain we owe some present-day

place names: Hochelaga was the Indian village Cartier visited in 1535 on the site of Montreal. (The word meant beaver dams.) The village disappeared before Champlain came, but the name is still used for the county that comprises the eastern part of the Island. To the hill behind Hochelaga, Cartier gave the name Mont-Royal. This was done in honour of Cardinal Hippolyte de Medici, Archbishop of Monreale (also spelled Montereale) in Sicily, who had been instrumental in securing papal sanction for the expedition. The first use of the present form, Montreal, was in 1635, when it was applied to the entire Island. Place Royale, on the riverfront, retains the name that Champlain gave in 1611 to this promising trading site. Champlain also left a place name for what is now Montreal's island park— Ile Ste-Hélène (St. Helen's Island), called so for the patron saint of his wife, Hélène.

VILLE MARIE

The settlement of 1642 was inspired by Christian missionary motives. It was an expression of the religious revival that swept France in the early seventeenth century. In 1640, a group of French men and women, the "Associés de Notre-Dame pour la conversion des sauvages de la Nouvelle France en l'île de Montréal," were made seigneurs, that is to say, manorial lords, of the Island of Montreal. On May 18, 1642, the first colonists sent out by the *Associés,* some fifty in number, landed. They established themselves on Place Royale, the riverside site so eulogized by Champlain, and commenced the mission settlement known as Ville Marie. This title, with its deeply religious connotation, was borne for about fifty years. As the original missionary motive was overlaid by others, the old title dropped out of use and was replaced by that of Montreal. Thus, Montreal, the name first given by Cartier in 1535 to the mountain (in the form of Mont-Royal), was applied in the 1630's to the Island, and finally, in the later 1680's, to the settlement.

The heroic, or founding, age extended over some twenty years (1642-63). The locale was the riverside; the purpose, to Christianize. The *Associés* found money and recruited settlers; in a word, maintained Ville Marie. The governor, Paul Chomedy, Sieur de Maisonneuve, was the model of the Christian soldier. One of his associates from the beginning was Jeanne Mance, who in 1644 founded the hospital, the Hôtel-Dieu. In the later 1650's, Marguerite Bourgeoys began teaching French and Indian children and thus carried forward the Christian, civilizing concept. Ville Marie surmounted the perils of settlement-planting in the wilderness and those of Indian wars. Its survival, in fact and in legend, provided the inspiration for later and less heroic ages.

THE
FUR-TRADING
COMMUNITY

Ville Marie was a mission post; early Montreal, a fur-trading centre. The change began imperceptibly. The Indian wars ceased with the reorganization of New France as a royal province in 1663. In the same year, the *Associés,* by this time old and reduced in numbers, transferred the settlement and all their seigneurial rights to the Seminary of Saint-Sulpice in Paris. Thus it fell to the Sulpicians to maintain the mission ideal, but in a new age. Each spring, flotillas of Indian canoes arrived, freighted with beaver pelts. A species of fair was held along the river shore or on the path that straggled between Place Royale and the Hôtel-Dieu. By the 1670's, a new settlement was growing up, back from the river, on the low hill now crowned by Place d'Armes. There, Montreal took shape on three long streets: St. Paul (the path mentioned before), Notre Dame, and St. James. The centre was Place d'Armes, where between 1672 and 1692 a church and a seminary (the latter actually a rectory and seigneury house) were built. The general director of this new develop-ment was Dollier de Casson, the Superior of the Sul-pician community in Montreal. He was the first town-planner; the regular street pattern of early Montreal (in contrast to that of Quebec or Boston) is a tribute to his skill.

A change in function underlay these new evidences of prosperity. By 1700, Montreal was no longer the scene of fur trading—the place of colourful Indian fairs —but the centre from which trade was organized. Fur was collected at distant western and northern posts such as Detroit and Sault Ste. Marie and then transferred to Montreal. The town was walled, for greater security, and much of it was honeycombed with deeply excavated vaults for the storage of the precious fur. An attempt was made to overcome one major disability of Montreal by the construction of a canal around the Lachine Rapids just west of the town. Like the modern St. Lawrence Seaway, the canal was to develop water power for mills. The canal was not fully completed, but that so much was done is a commentary on the economic vigour of early Montreal.

While Montreal was on the frontier, it was not a typical frontier town. There was much that was crude and raw; nevertheless, it provided a wide range of social services. For occasional relief, there was the Bureau des Pauvres (1684); for the permanent care of the destitute, the Hôpital-Général (1741). Schools for boys and girls were maintained by Sulpicians and Jesuits and by the Ladies of the Congregation of Notre Dame, the foundation of Marguerite Bourgeoys herself. Even the Indian, the forgotten man elsewhere in America, was provided with mission settlements at Oka and Caughnawaga.

THE ERA
OF
REVOLUTION
1760-1817

It was this community, generally stable and well-established, that experienced three momentous upheavals in the middle and late eighteenth century. The first was the cession of French Canada to Britain

4

in 1763. The other two were the American and French revolutions. Singly and together the three events profoundly affected Montreal and its later history. In contrast to these three, the War of 1812-14 was scarcely felt in Montreal.

The Cession

An especial interest surrounds Montreal's share in the Cession. It was in Montreal on September 8, 1760, that the Governor of New France signed the capitulation that virtually ended French rule in North America. For almost a year following the surrender of Quebec to the British (September 18, 1759), Montreal was the capital of Canada. The Governor, the Marquis de Vaudreuil, and his officials took up residence in Montreal, occupying the "Intendancy," a building that stood on St. Paul Street at the foot of the Bonsecours market. Bishop Pontbriand lived with the Sulpicians and died in May 1760 in a little room in the Seminary. Montreal found the supplies and military stores for the last defence of French Canada. It was from Montreal that the Chevalier de Lévis left in April 1760 to win the second battle of the Plains of Abraham (April 28), otherwise known as the battle of Ste-Foy. Ste-Foy was, however, a Pyrrhic victory, since the Canadians and French did not possess the resources for a siege of Quebec. The arrival of an English relieving fleet compelled a withdrawal to Montreal.

At Montreal, the defenders awaited the slow converging of the British armies. In reality, the town was hardly defensible. The wall had fallen into disrepair and, furthermore, was overlooked by the high ground of modern Beaver Hall Hill. Even when the outlying garrisons were drawn in, Lévis had only some 3,500 men, badly armed and starving. Desertion was rife, especially among the country militia. An attempt was made to turn St. Helen's Island into a stronghold. Trenches were dug and batteries sited to dispute the passage of the St. Mary's Current. Early in September, before much could be done, the British arrived—three armies, in all over 16,000 men. The French military, Lévis and his officers, were for making a last stand on St. Helen's Island, leaving Montreal to be defended by the townspeople and the militia. Vaudreuil countermanded the plan, and, on September 7, negotiations for the surrender were begun. The capitulation was signed in the early hours of September 8, 1760. It provided for the surrender of Montreal, the garrison and government officials, and the surrender of the western posts. Thus, while New France could survive the loss of Quebec by nearly a year, the loss of Montreal carried with it the loss of the entire colony.

The formalities of the capitulation were carried out on September 9. The French and Canadian troops paraded on Place d'Armes, where they laid down their arms. A British force took possession of the Récollet gate, entered the town, and raised its flag on the citadel at the eastern end of Montreal. In the course of the next few days, the Marquis de Vaudreuil, his officials, and the French military left Montreal. At about the same time, small expeditions were sent westward to receive the surrender of the trading posts in the upper country. A miniature British force also went eastward to a fortified position on the Jacques Cartier River (the site of modern Donnacona), where the French still held out. With the submission of this post, the terms of the capitulation of Montreal became operative over all New France. Three years later, the Treaty of Paris transferred Canada to Britain. In negotiating the treaty, France preferred to give up Canada and keep her sugar islands.

The Cession brought Montreal the problems of a new allegiance, a new race relationship, and a new trading position.   In considering allegiance and race relationships, two factors are of importance. The first to remember is that in the 1760's the cult of nationality was not strong, while the cult of monarchy was. French Canadians who had been dutiful subjects of King Louis could become dutiful subjects of King George. Change of allegiance was a situation the eighteenth century understood perfectly. It saw Spain give allegiance to a French king, Naples to a Spanish king, and England to a German. In the instance of French Canada, it was *l'accession à la couronne britannique.* Secondly, during the campaign of 1760, Montreal endured little material damage; it experienced no atrocities.[3] Few Montrealers appear to have withdrawn to France, as they were entitled to do under the terms of the capitulation and the subsequent Treaty of Paris. Those who stayed were assured of continued ownership of their property, whether private or corporate. The Sulpicians remained, and the continuance of this great religious corporation, which was at the same time the greatest landholder in Montreal, was of enormous consequence. (The Sulpicians' legal position as a Canadian institution was established in 1764, when the title and seigneurial rights of the Sulpicians of Paris were transferred to their community in Montreal.) Although they were to provoke discussion at a later time, the rights of the Montreal Sulpicians were never seriously challenged. Their services—religious, educational, and charitable—continued in the new dispensation.

For twenty years or more after the Cession, the conquerors formed an infinitesimal part of the population and were not readily distinguishable from it. It was not till 1776 that they erected a place of worship for themselves. This was a synagogue built by the Jewish members of the group.[4] Since the newcomers were all traders (apart from a handful of civilian administrators and military men), they were dependent on the good will of the established French or French Canadians. The language of commerce was French, and the English merchants were, or rapidly became, bilingual. More subtle forces were at work. The registers of the first regularly appointed Anglican clergyman in Montreal (himself an old-country Frenchman) show that of the five hundred marriages he solemnized between 1766 and 1794 over a quarter were between English men and French-Canadian women.[5] In the literal sense, therefore, the mother tongue of the growing part of "English" Montreal was French.

The Cession created acute economic problems for Montreal. These caused more disruption of life than did the change of allegiance or the new race relationship. Montreal had to accommodate itself to the breaking of the old commercial ties with France and to the formation of new ties with Britain. This accommodation was far from complete when Montreal became entangled in the American Revolution.

The American Revolution

The American Revolution added further complications: it led to the occupation of Montreal by the Americans in 1775-76.[5] Probably the impact of the event was lessened by the Quebec Act of 1774. This measure had opened official careers to French Canadians. Furthermore, it insured a degree of legal establishment for the Roman Catholic Church. In Montreal, the conservative elements that gave the cold shoulder to the Americans were as much French as English.[7] The Sulpicians were conspicuous in their upholding of royal authority. Conversely, a number of English-speaking merchants ranged themselves among "the friends of Congress," and some left the city with the retreating Americans in the summer of 1776. They were replaced by American royalists, some of whom, such as Sir John Johnson, became life-long residents. A number of refugee American clergy ministered in Montreal. One of these, the Reverend John Bethune, became the founder of the first Presbyterian congregation.[8] Finally, some merchants, chiefly from New York or Albany, settled in Montreal in order to pursue the fur trade. The newcomers were anything but self-effacing. They placed a check on the assimilation of the English that had been going on since the Cession. The irony of the situation was that, although they were usually described as "English," the most numerous were Americans or Irish, and the most conspicuous, Scots. The representative figures of early English Montreal answered to such un-English names as James McGill and Simon McTavish.

The French Revolution

The French Revolution caused a drawing together of the possessing classes. In the 1790's, the Montreal Sulpicians received twelve *émigrés* from their Paris community. French-Canadian magistrates, no less than English, were alarmed by the popular resistance to governmental interference in everyday life; for example, to the Road Act of 1796 and to the embodying of the militia in 1794. The Road Act imposed a tax or statute labour for extensive road improvement in Lower Canada; the militia act demanded registration by the male population for possible calling to service in the defence of the province. As late as 1812, fear and opposition were the response to the calling out of the militia. The well-to-do of both racial groups found common ground in making contributions to patriotic funds, and in raising at least one monument to ideological solidarity—the Nelson column at the head of the Bonsecours Market.

The New Economy

The French and American revolutions completed the change in Montreal's economic position begun by the Cession. Montreal was left as the only major trading centre in British North America, its rivals, New York, Albany, and the New England towns, having joined in secession. In the future, Montreal could describe its commercial ambitions in patriotic national terms. Montreal also adopted a proprietary interest in the St. Lawrence route to Europe. A generation or so later, publicists would enlarge on the possibilities of "the commercial empire of the St. Lawrence." In material terms, the American Revolution damaged the fur trade, by jeopardizing Montreal's trade route by way of the Great Lakes and by depriving it of its trading area south of the Lakes. The plan of the Montreal association, the Northwest Company, to open a new area by a new route, the Ottawa Valley, was economically unsound, although it was pursued until 1821. Long before that date, the French Revolution (by threatening England's economic connection with the Baltic) had drawn Montreal into other lines of trade: the export of wood-ash, square timber, and cereals. "The new staple trades," as they were called, sustained early nineteenth-century Montreal.

The new staples went far towards producing a new Montreal. Even before the end of the eighteenth century, they encouraged changes in transportation and finance. Barge canals appeared on the upper St. Lawrence, and a toll road, the Lachine turnpike, was built (between 1804 and 1805) on the Island of Montreal itself. The proprietors of the road were said to have made a fortune during the War of 1812-14, when the British government paid more in tolls for freight than would have been required to build an adequate canal. An attempt to bridge the channel between the east end of the Island and the mainland was defeated when two successive bridges, built by the Seigneur of Terrebonne (Thomas Porteous), were swept away by ice. A bank, to be known as the Canada Banking Company, was projected. (The bank, which did not materialize, was to be a private, not a public, bank. It is not to be confused with the private bank of somewhat similar name that existed briefly in the early nineteenth century, or with the modern Bank of Canada.) These were clear foreshadowings of the next century, when Montreal would become the centre of canals, roads, and railways and the centre of banking as well. In 1817, Canada's first bank was established. It was named (how appropriately!) the Bank of Montreal.

2 HOPES RAISED BY STEAM

Montreal's life depended upon the use of the St. Lawrence not only as a possible route but as a preferred route for the transportation of the new staples. Although local publicists were tireless in their praise, the river was a qualified blessing.[1] It was closed by winter for four or five months of the year, and even when open it presented difficulties. East of Montreal were tortuous channels and shallows, as, for example, in Lake St. Peter; in the lower river and gulf were racing currents. West of Montreal, rapids extended to Cornwall, some ninety miles away. Even Lake Ontario was a *cul de sac,* since its western end was blocked by rapids and falls in the Niagara River. Nor did the northern and southern tributaries of the St. Lawrence, the Ottawa and the Richelieu, provide open channels to the hinterland. So long as Montreal's main commodity was fur, high in value and small in bulk, these disadvantages were not serious. When, however, bulky wood-ash, timber, and cereals became the staples, the shortcomings of the St. Lawrence route were shown in high relief. The rise of the new staples coincided with intensified competition from Montreal's old rival, New York. In addition to its natural advantages of a milder climate and immediate access to the sea, New York acquired canal connection (1825) westward to Lake Erie, the heart of the Great Lakes region. Montrealers believed that river improvement and, above all, the application of steam to transportation would restore the balance.

River improvement consisted chiefly in the construction of barge canals. This was carried on over a long period and under a variety of authorities. The earliest effort was made in 1779 at Coteau du Lac (about forty miles west of Montreal) by the provincial government. A later canal was built at Beauharnois, through the enterprise of the seigneur, Edward Ellice. The last (and nearest) canal was the Lachine. It was begun by the Montreal merchants themselves, who in 1819 formed a canal company, but it was completed by the provincial government of Lower Canada in 1826.[2]

The harbour also enlisted attention. It was walled with wood near the canal entrance, and gaps in the wall allowed for sloping roadways down to the river level.[3] Improvement and extension of this primitive facility caused constant anxiety to the Montreal merchants; in the 1840's granite replaced wood, and ramps, built down into the harbour along the side of a now continuous wall, replaced the sloping roads; shallow basins were hollowed out along the shore for ships to lie in while receiving or discharging cargoes. As piers were built, the harbour began to extend out into the river. In 1821, in order to drive forward harbour improvement, the merchants formed the Committee of Trade (later called the Board of Trade), the oldest and probably the most influential trade association in Montreal.

The improvement of the river channel below the city, while of vital concern to Montrealers, was carried on by the provincial government of Lower Canada.[4] Nevertheless, Montreal's right to representation was recognized when, in 1830, a body of Montreal Harbour Commissioners was appointed. (The Montreal representatives were named at first by the Committee of Trade, and later by the Board of Trade and the city council.) The Harbour Commissioners continued under the government of the Province of Canada. This organization, along with the earlier one known as Trinity House (whose responsibility was limited to licensing pilots), may be regarded as the forerunner of the modern National Harbours Board.

High hopes were placed on the application of steam to navigation.[5] In November 1809, John Molson, the Montreal brewer and pioneer industrialist, sent the first steam river boat, the *Accommodation,* down to Quebec. It had been built and equipped in Montreal—a commentary on the advanced character of the city in technology. Fifteen years later (1824), the first towboat (appropriately named the *Hercules*) was put into service to draw shipping upstream from Quebec to Montreal. The *Hercules,* and later towboats, mastered the St. Mary's Current. This was the devastating current that began above St. Helen's Island and made movement into and within the port of Montreal so dangerous. The steam boats also mastered the prevailing winds, which, blowing from the west, caused sail shipping to lie wind-bound for weeks on Lake St. Peter.

In 1840, steam won a spectacular victory, when the *Ontario,* brought down by Jacques Oteronhiare, a Caughnawaga pilot, demonstrated that a steamship could descend the Lachine Rapids. Steam vessels (which at that time had side paddle wheels) could be steered through an intricate channel in a way that a sailing vessel could not. However, even steam could not take the steep rise of the ascent. Until the Lachine Canal was enlarged, in the late 1840's, steamships from the lower St. Lawrence stopped at Montreal; those from the west, at Lachine—unless they were intended thereafter for service below Montreal. After the Lachine Canal was enlarged, it was the normal route for shipping going both ways, but for the next ninety years shooting the rapids by steamer was still possible. Until the late 1930's, the Canada Steamship Lines maintained two vessels for the express purpose of giving people this thrill.

Steam gave impetus to Montreal as a ship-building centre—for marine engines as well as for the vessels themselves. The *Royal William* was built in Quebec and towed to Montreal to have its engine installed. On leaving, it met with a misfortune less fatal than the report would suggest: "The *Royal William* grounded near Montreal, while descending the river . . . all attempts to get her off have failed." The *Royal William* not only survived this adventure: in 1833 it became the first ship to cross the Atlantic using steam as the principal driving force.

The early railways in the Montreal area were auxiliaries of the rivers. In 1836, the first of them was built to provide easy communication between the St. Lawrence and the navigable sections of the Richelieu. Eleven years later (1847), the first railway on the Island of Montreal was constructed to give speedy transportation around the Lachine Rapids.

THE
GRAND TRUNK
ERA

The full impact of the railway on Montreal began with the chartering of the Grand Trunk in 1853. This company had purchased the St. Lawrence and Atlantic, which ran from Longueuil (on the south shore of the St. Lawrence, just east of Montreal) to Portland. It intended to build a new line to Sarnia, and, once the river was spanned, to provide uninterrupted "trunk" service from the Atlantic seaboard. Although other factors contributed to the good times—the Crimean War and the Reciprocity Treaty—the railway gave Montreal its earliest industrial boom. The Grand Trunk era carried Montreal into and far beyond Confederation.

Materials for railway building were assembled at Montreal, and the shops required for servicing the line were located there. The Grand Trunk introduced a cadre of highly skilled workers, who became the schoolmasters of a generation of young Montrealers working as apprentices in the great shops at Pointe St. Charles. The shops were, therefore, advanced technical institutes of enormous consequence to the modern development of the city.

It was at Montreal that the railway undertook its greatest single enterprise, the building of the Victoria Bridge. A bridge across the St. Lawrence was essential, if the railway was to provide continuous transportation. Its location was a matter of the most intense interest. The site finally selected was Pointe St. Charles, from which the bridge was carried across to St. Lambert. Building went forward between 1854 and 1859, giving employment to about seven thousand men.[6] The 9,184-foot bridge was built of iron plates and was tubular in design, the form favoured by Robert Stephenson, the English engineer who built it. In December 1859 it was completed, and, on December 17, the Grand Trunk entrained a party for the first ride across it. However, before the merrymakers entered the great iron tube, their train was halted to allow the passage of a freight, loaded with cotton bales from Cairo (Illinois) en route to New England. The bridge was opened formally in August 1860 by the Prince of Wales, the future Edward VII.

In October 1856, before the bridge was completed, the Grand Trunk sponsored a three-day "Railway Celebration" to mark the opening of the line from Montreal to Toronto. On October 28, a grand procession perambulated Montreal. Its various elements gave an accurate notion of Montreal at the dawn of the new age—the Montreal of the artisan. Industry was represented by the traditional skilled trades: carpentry, printing, shoemaking, blacksmithing, and so on. The master workmen and journeymen, dressed in the costumes associated with their crafts, marched under the banners of their benefit societies. The Agricultural Society was conspicuous (an indication of the close relationship between town and countryside); its banner displayed an idyllic scene, the Garden of Eden, over the motto "The First Occupation of Man." Another part of the celebration had a most unusual location. The banquet was laid in the Grand Trunk shops in Pointe St. Charles. A gala ball was held in the Bonsecours Market House, which served as the city hall and general civic centre. Some six thousand persons attended; so it is not surprising that great damage was done to the hoops of many ladies' dresses. At various times during the three days of festivity, a patriotic locomotive rendered "God Save the Queen" on its whistle.

Unfortunately, the Grand Trunk did not greatly benefit from these costly exercises in public relations. What is even more surprising is the speed with which the railway became the object of widespread dislike. Management was in Britain and had the character of an absentee landlord, indifferent and impervious to complaint. The travelling public was irritated by having to go to Pointe St. Charles to meet trains, there being no city station till 1862. Shippers were enraged by what they considered discriminatory freight rates: since they were in the middle, Montrealers shipped over relatively short distances and therefore paid at the maximum rate. They also considered it unfair that rates were raised at the close of navigation, when the railway had a monopoly. Finally, they complained about the lethargy displayed in laying track to the Montreal waterfront. Carters, too, had a grievance: the railway gave an exclusive contract to its own forwarding agent, Sheddon and Company. The Grand Trunk earned the enmity of publicists; of none more than of Thomas C. Keefer. He was a Canadian civil engineer and a tireless writer on transportation problems. Keefer had early projected a St. Lawrence bridge, in location and design, similar to the Victoria. The Grand Trunk, however, jilted him in favour of Stephenson and thus earned Keefer's lifelong hostility.[7] By the decade of Confederation, the railway had succeeded in turning public opinion against itself.

THE
PORT

I n contrast to the railway, the port and shipping enjoyed sustained goodwill.[8] The harbour improvements begun at an earlier time were now completed, and their benefits were easy to see. The basins and the harbour wall provided satisfactory dockage; the deepening of the river channel below Montreal, and of the canals above, brought increasing shipping.[9] Following Britain's suspension of her Navigation Laws in 1847, foreign shipping (in contrast to British or colonial) began to enter the port. On June 2, 1847, a little German vessel, flying the scarlet and white checkerboard flag of the free city of Bremen, reached Montreal. This marked a new stage in Montreal's (and Canada's) economic emancipation. The schooner *New Brunswick* cleared Montreal in late May 1847. She was the first ship to come down the lakes and canals from Chicago. Early in 1853, there was another sensation, the arrival of the *Glenova,* the first steam vessel from overseas. A civic reception was clearly in order. It cost Montrealers £249.4s.11d., perhaps not an extravagant price in view of what the steamship was to mean to the fortunes of the city. In 1855 two ships of the greatest interest were in the port. In July, *La Capricieuse* reached Montreal, the first French war vessel to do so since the Cession. In November, a brig came in from Sydney, New South Wales. She was the first vessel to reach Montreal from the Antipodes.

Effective use of the port was made by Hugh Allan. He formed the Montreal Ocean Steamship Company, which in 1855 undertook a regular service to the British Isles. Thus Allan did for Montreal what Samuel Cunard had done for Halifax. Both ventures owed their success to government subsidies, which were provided for the carriage of mail. In the instance of Allan, the money came, before 1867, from the Province of Canada; after Confederation, from the federal government. The Allan Line, as the corporation was usually called, made Montreal an Atlantic port—the realization of many dreams. This practical consideration, along with the more sentimental one of Allan's personal identification with Montreal, helps to account for the enormous popularity of everything connected with the river, shipping, and the harbour. When G. M. Grant commissioned the illustrations for his monumental *Picturesque Canada,* his artist depicted the waterfront for the frontispiece of the section on Montreal. The most conspicuous feature was an Allan liner.

3 NINETEENTH-CENTURY MONTREAL

The outstanding feature of Montreal life in the first sixty years of the century was population growth. Population shot up from about 18,000 in 1821 to over 91,000 in 1861, and to an estimated 100,000 at Confederation. Five or six Montrealers stood where there had been one forty-six years before. Much of the increase was derived from the British Isles. Thus was produced the interesting phenomenon of an English-speaking majority in Montreal between the middle 1840's and at least 1861. Capital and technical skills accompanied the large-scale movement of population from the British Isles and were factors in civic growth. The basic one was, however, the crowding in of people.

THE IMMIGRANT TIDE

British immigration began with the ending of the French Revolutionary and Napoleonic wars in 1815 and continued to beyond the mid-century. The first wave came with the disbanding of the wartime army and navy, and rose to a peak in 1819. The second wave, in the 1830's, reflected hard times in Europe, and the third, in the 1840's, was the result of the potato famine in Ireland.

The newcomers of the first wave were largely Scots and English. Some were relatively well-to-do. There is a striking description of one group, as they marched up from the steamboat wharf below the Bonsecours Chapel behind a piper, "clad in the garb of old Gaul [Gael] playing national music." Others were very poor; many, indeed, destitute, as records of various charitable organizations, the Ladies' Benevolent Society or the Christ Church Committee of Managers . . . for the Poor, bear witness.

In the 1830's, Irish joined with the Scots and the English. Almost all were of the prosperous classes. In fact this group contained many men who, twenty years or so later, were to give Montreal a continental name. For the moment, they were happy to make Montreal over to their liking.

The third immigrant wave, which came in the late 1840's, was overwhelmingly Irish—the famine migration. The failure of the potato crop, which began in 1845, produced panic-flight by 1847. In the summer of that year, immigrants poured into Montreal, nearly all destitute, many starving and disease-ridden. Typhus accompanied the famine sufferers. The consequences were appalling to the Irish themselves and to the Montrealers who ministered to them. Of the latter, the clergy and their lay helpers were the heaviest sufferers. The most conspicuous victim was the mayor, John Easton Mills. He had initially opposed public relief measures, since he feared that they would take the place of private responsibility. Mills's natural generosity finally got the better of his free-enterprise principles, and he died, attempting to undo the damage he had done. Children left destitute by their parents' death were adopted by kindly Montrealers, many of them French Canadians. For a long time, the *enfants de Pointe-Saint-Charles* kept alive the memory of 1847. "The Immigrant Stone," which stands near the north end of the Victoria Bridge, was set up by the workmen who built the bridge as a memorial to the thousands of immigrants who were buried nearby.

ORGANIZATION

Sheer numbers made necessary a degree of organization unknown before. In 1833, Montreal was incorporated and endowed with a measure of local self-government. (See next chapter.) Ecclesiastical organization was another important development.

Official church recognition for the Montreal area was achieved first by the Roman Catholics, for whom the Diocese of Montreal was created in 1836. Fifteen years earlier (1821), a preliminary step had been taken. The Reverend Jean-Jacques Lartigue was consecrated Bishop of Telmesse and suffragan or assistant to the Bishop of Quebec to administer the Montreal district. Bishop Lartigue's position was not an easy one. His authority was limited; his resources, small. In the figurative as well as in the literal sense, he lived in the shadow of the Seminary, whose members, as seigneur, still controlled the finances of the Island of Montreal. It was not till 1825 that he was provided with a cathedral, when St-Jacques-le-Majeur was built at the corner of St. Denis and St. Catherine streets. Only in 1836 did he attain the full dignity of Bishop of Montreal, when the British government finally withdrew its objection to the use of the title. Bishop Lartigue did not long enjoy his new prosperity, for he died in 1840. The second bishop, Ignace Bourget (1841-76), was one of the great figures of this and of the post-Confederation era.[1]

Other communions were slower in organizing, probably because their numbers were smaller. In 1850, the Anglican Diocese of Montreal was set up. By that date, every major religious denomination was represented in Montreal. The larger had more than one place of worship: Roman Catholics and Anglicans, four churches each; Presbyterians, three; Methodists, two; Jews, two. Baptists, Congregationalists, and Unitarians had one each. The churches and synagogues were all situated in or near what today would be called old Montreal—the area bounded by Craig, McGill, and Berri streets.

On all denominations the care of the sick and the destitute and the provision of schooling for children pressed heavily. Roman Catholics made great use of religious orders. In the 1840's, Bishop Bourget introduced five: Jesuits, Oblates of Mary Immaculate, Brothers of the Christian Schools, Sisters of Providence, and Sisters of Mercy. Non-Roman Catholics had nothing comparable to offer, but they attempted to meet their responsibilities by co-operative effort. A very successful one produced the Montreal General Hospital, which received its first patients in 1822.[2] About twenty years later (1843), the problem of securing a good secondary school for boys yielded to the same solution—common action among various English-speaking groups—and the High School of Montreal was successfully started. Later, the government scholarships of the old Royal Grammar School (1818-43) were directed to it.[3] In 1852, an amended charter for McGill University freed the Board of Governors of its exclusively Anglican character and thus carried co-operation into the field of higher education. Earliest McGill had been dominated by Anglicans, a reflection of the Church-State relationship that had placed the appointment of the governors in the hands of what was in practice an Anglican body. The amended charter declared that the governors should be laymen from various Protestant denominations and should be residents of Montreal.

TENSIONS

Numbers generated tensions. These became acute in times of economic distress, or in periods of panic occasioned by epidemic disease. The first major epidemic, that of cholera in 1832, preceded the election riot of that year. The Montreal phases of the Rebellion of 1837 were closely associated with the commercial depression; the disorders of 1849, with the business collapse of 1846 and with the typhus of 1847. The cholera of 1852 was followed by the Gavazzi Riot of 1853. In this disturbance, the split was on a religious basis; in others it might have followed racial lines. The national societies of the middle 1830's, St. Patrick's, St. Andrew's, St-Jean-Baptiste, and St. George's, sharpened racial consciousness. Until the early 1850's, these organizations were active political agencies, regimenting the masses and providing ladders for the ambitious. (Compare Chapter 5.)

Tensions were increased by political strains. In 1840, Lower and Upper Canada were united to form the Province of Canada, of which Montreal was, in 1843, made the political capital. It was already the commercial capital; so there was logic in the choice. Moreover, occupying the Tom Tiddler's ground between French and English, Montreal could claim to satisfy both. The city council readily leased the St. Anne's Market, and it was here that Parliament met in 1844. It met in Montreal for the last time in 1849. In the course of rioting, the immediate cause of which was the Rebellion Losses Bill, the Parliament House was burned and the Governor General hunted out of Montreal. The disturbances of 1849 cost Montreal its brief fame as the capital of Canada.

"DISMEMBERMENT" OF THE PARISH OF MONTREAL

Tensions also disturbed one of the oldest institutions in Montreal. The Parish of Montreal, the ecclesiastical administrative unit, dated back to 1660.[4] In 1678, it was formally established by Bishop Laval, who placed it under the charge of the Sulpicians. The Church of Notre Dame on Place d'Armes was the parish church of Montreal, *la paroisse.* It was there that registers were kept, baptisms performed, marriages celebrated, and burial services held. Other churches, such as St. Patrick's and St-Jacques-le-Majeur, were in the nature of chapels, subordinate to the parish church. They were intended only for worship; legal or official aspects of church life had to be transacted at *la paroisse.* (The chapels of the religious communities, such as that of the nuns of the Hôtel-Dieu, were not, ordinarily, open to public use.) In the period of rapid population growth, the situation became thoroughly unsatisfactory. Bishop Bourget determined on "the dismemberment," as it was alarmingly called, of the ancient parish of Montreal. The ensuing controversy swept in about every element of the Roman Catholic community, including the two Confederation fathers, George-Etienne Cartier and Thomas D'Arcy McGee, both of whom opposed the division. In 1865, the Bishop had his way, and in 1866 and 1867 the first divisions of the parish were made. In anticipation,

St. Patrick's and the Cathedral (St-Jacques-le-Majeur) began to keep registers in 1859 and 1862 respectively.

Bishop Bourget's decision had sweeping secular consequences. Montrealers were encouraged to move freely, knowing that parishes would be created as population warranted, and that these would be legally competent to serve the people. It is a fair assumption that a good deal of the outward movement of the post-Confederation period may be traced to the loosening of rigidities in 1865. A second decentralizing force set in, in 1876, when the Quebec provincial government enacted its law of municipal corporations (40 Victoria, cap. 49). This measure allowed parishes to become incorporated as civil municipalities. A number of parishes in the neighbourhood of Montreal took advantage of the act and became autonomous political units. Some of these, for example Notre Dame de Grâce, were absorbed later by Montreal; others remained autonomous, for example Verdun and Westmount. Thus the tensions leading to the division of the historic parish of Montreal had consequences that extended far beyond the decade of the 1860's.[5]

Change and adaptibility to change were written large in the early history of Montreal. The mission station, in altered circumstances, became a centre of education and of social service. The town, without surrendering its French inheritance, expanded to include the English-speaking newcomers. The trading post at the foot of the rapids became the metropolis of the new nation created by Confederation.

4 MUNICIPAL GOVERNMENT

PART I: THE ART OF THE POSSIBLE

Municipal government is one of the oldest arts to be practised in Montreal. Under one form or another, it has existed since Maisonneuve's time. In range, however, it is severely limited, since the city is the subject of an external authority that determines the degree of its autonomy. Practical limitations have been imposed, as well, by the much-divided nature of Montreal's population: vested interests have been strongly entrenched; prejudices, easy to rouse. In spite of the experience of over two hundred years, until about twenty years after Confederation, Montreal government was cautious almost to the extent of being rooted.

A LENGTHY LOOK BEHIND

The inclination to accept authority from above was a temper that was slow to die. It was Montreal's primary misfortune to be born at the height of royal absolutism, the seventeenth century, when kings restricted the powers of their cities and appointed their governors. (Three hundred years before, kings had been anxious to extend the autonomy of their cities.) Maisonneuve and his successors, governors of Montreal, were appointed by *Messieurs les Associés* till 1663 and after that date by the Sovereign Council of Quebec, in both instances, in the name of the king. The governor appointed a local man, called a syndic, to be a spokesman for his fellow citizens. The Montreal governor promulgated ordinances for the regulation of city life. Maisonneuve, for example, issued ten ordinances on such varied subjects as the defence of the town, the sale of intoxicants, and the building of the church.[1] The Montreal governor, however, was overshadowed by the Governor of New France, who almost every year came to Montreal and issued his own ordinances. In 1674, Montrealers lost their right to have a syndic, and so had no means of objecting to outside authority. The régime was accepted with resignation. Only twice before 1763 was there protest: in 1704 and 1705, there were riots provoked by the high price of salt.

Shortly after the Cession there was a change. In Britain, in spite of absolutism, the tradition of local government had remained strong, especially in the country districts. There administration was carried out by justices of the peace (often called magistrates), who, although they were appointed, were nevertheless local people. In 1764, this type of administration was introduced into Montreal. (From 1760, the British had employed a Montreal governor, but the office was discontinued with the appointment of the magistrates.) Twenty-seven justices sat weekly, two by two, in rotation. For sixty-nine years, that is to say, until 1833, the justices of the peace ruled Montreal. Their regulations extended over all phases of city life.[2] They forbade empty carriages to stand in the market-place. They directed that owners of swine should ring the creatures' noses "to hinder them rooting up [the] high roads." The magistrates determined the weight of bread and the charges that ferrymen might make.

In 1799, the powers of the magistrates were greatly extended by legislation of the parliament of Lower Canada. The measure (36 George III, cap. 5) increased the number of magistrates and empowered them to collect taxes and to hold elections for minor posts. The magistrates thus came to form a genuine government in the modern sense. The justices continued to meet weekly and began to hold formal sessions four times a year in what were called "courts of quarter session." They undertook responsibility for the upkeep of streets and for the safeguarding of public health. The first cholera visitation, in 1832, spurred action: garbage was to be collected and disposed of; pigs were discouraged from frequenting public places (so, there was no repetition of the homely occasion when a pig entered the Bank of Montreal to scratch its back). A watch, or police force of sorts, was recruited, armed with rattles and long blue staffs. Finally, the justices of the peace recognized their own limitations: as early as 1826, they petitioned parliament to set up representative municipal institutions and to end their own rule.[3]

THE EARLY
ELECTIVE REGIME

The new régime came into operation in June 1833, by virtue of an act of incorporation accorded by the parliament of Lower Canada. Montreal's population was then about thirty-one thousand. (The following year, York with a population of about nine thousand was incorporated as the City of Toronto.) The measure had been enacted in 1831, but it was not proclaimed until two years later, an unpleasant foretaste of the dilatoriness often observable in Montreal's contact with the legislature. The essential feature of the measure was the election of a city council by the property owners. Thus, the right of the citizens to choose their own governors was at last recognized—after nearly two hundred years. The administrative powers of the council were restricted to the city itself, and its financial powers were limited to local taxation or to borrowing up to a fraction of the assessed value of property. Finally, the life span of the charter of incorporation was fixed at four years. These limitations clearly show the subordination of the municipality to the provincial legislature and the unreality of its autonomy.

Montreal's first civic election, held in June 1833, was a very tame affair. In seven of the eight wards there was no contest at all, and in the eighth (stormy St. Anne's) only eighty-four of an eligible 118 voters met to choose two out of three candidates. In the eyes of the Montreal Tories, the election marked the beginning of the reign of "King Mob." The council held its first meeting on June 5, when it elected the historian Jacques Viger as mayor. In 1836, the act of incorporation expired, since the provincial parliament had neglected to renew it. (This was probably the result of the chaos in government preceding the Rebellion of 1837.) Rule by magistrates was resumed. In 1840, a new charter was granted, but the mayor and councillors were to be appointed by the provincial government. In 1843, the elective principle was completely restored.[4]

In the twenty-four years between 1843 and 1867, the scope and the activity of the city council greatly increased. The most important single step was the purchase by the municipality of the privately owned water system. This was done in 1845 for the price of £50,000. The council thereby took on a service character. Between 1852 and 1856, the city constructed an entirely new water supply system. Water was drawn from the St. Lawrence above the Lachine Rapids, brought by means of an aqueduct to a point on modern Atwater Avenue, and then pumped to reservoirs on the side of Mount Royal. (The engineer in charge of the undertaking was Thomas C. Keefer, railway promoter, bridge designer, and McGill's first lecturer in engineering. It was he who supervised the construction of waterworks in other cities, for example in Toronto, when in 1874 that city also bought out a private company.) The waterworks purchase and subsequent enlargement launched the city government on its modern course. Pure water was vital to public health; an adequate supply of water, to public safety (for fire protection) and to industrial development. The great fires of 1852 were a terrible lesson, pointing to the necessity of modernizing Montreal's water system. The borrowing by the city of money to meet the cost of the improvements opened a fresh chapter in its experience. A the same time, Montreal borrowed in order to extend credit to various railway projects and so further increased its indebtedness. The point to be observed is the enormous increase in the activity and the responsibility of city administration.[5]

In this period, otherwise so loaded with positive achievement, there was one notable backward step. In 1852, the mayor began to be elected directly by the enfranchised citizens and not by the city council as heretofore (except for the period 1840 to 1842, when all were appointed by the provincial government). There appears to have been no general demand for the elective mayoralty, and in retrospect the change must be regarded as unfortunate. Mayor and council divided authority, but with no clearly defined spheres. The mayor had no means of inducing the council to follow his lead. Any influence he had was through the accident of popularity. Montreal secured for itself many of the disabilities of irresponsible government, as so much of the history of city administration was to show.

The story of municipal government is continued in Chapter 11.

5 ON THE EVE OF CONFEDERATION

Montrealers' support of Confederation reflected a fact, a mood, and a fear.

Manifold increase in population, such as Montreal experienced in the first sixty years of the nineteenth century, had been repeated elsewhere: the total population for British North America had gone from about 400,000 at the beginning of the century to over 3,000,000 in 1861. These same figures, multiplied by ten in each case, were approximately true for the United States. Increased population had meant increased cargoes (still propelled largely by sail) coming down the Lachine Canal, and increased business for the mills and factories that had grown up around the locks at St. Gabriel and Côte St. Paul, where surplus water could be leased. As early as 1847, an enterprising New Englander, Ira Gould, had opened the City Flour Mill, the pioneer undertaking. In the 1850's, Gould had successful imitators: John Redpath, with a sugar factory, and Alexander and John Ogilvie, with a second flour mill. As described in Chapter 2, the Grand Trunk Railway, chartered in 1853, put up its shops and erecting-sheds on the promontory known as Pointe St. Charles, Montreal's first industrial suburb, and constructed the Victoria Bridge, the greatest single industrial undertaking in nineteenth-century Montreal. In 1856, as part of the celebrations marking the opening of railway connection with Toronto, a group of Montrealers published a brochure outlining the progress of their city in the decade.[1] It seemed to be enjoying the first period of sustained good times since the 1820's. One single factor more than any other was responsible for their return: the ratification, in 1854, of the trade treaty with the United States known as the Reciprocity Treaty. This gave free entry to natural products and so allowed Montreal to capitalize fully upon the increase in population and the improvements in water and land transportation.

The upward curve of prosperity was expressed in the appearance of the city. We have a clearer picture of Montreal at this stage than at any earlier. Many buildings of the 1850's and 1860's still stand. In addition, there is a wealth of illustration, the camera having come to supplement the canvas or the engraving-block of the graphic recorder. It was in the later 1850's that William Notman began his career as a commercial photographer. Although Notman was interested more in Montrealers than in Montreal, he included pictures of buildings and some street scenes. These show the city as the citizens liked to think it was—dignified and orderly. The *Illustrated London News* also provided views of Montreal; the visit of the Prince of Wales in 1860 was well documented pictorially.

On Advent Sunday, 1859, the new Christ Church Cathedral on Phillips Square was first used for worship. This fine gothic structure was not only a landmark in public taste; it was a finger post to the northwest movement of population.[2] By that date, or a year or so later, both Sherbrooke and St. Catherine streets had attracted the house builder. In 1860, the Prince of Wales Terrace on the north side of Sherbrooke Street was built. It was the largest of its kind in Montreal, and, like the cathedral, a landmark. The terrace had already established itself as a favourite choice of Montreal builders. In the rebuilding that followed the fire of 1845 and the enormous conflagrations of 1852, these dwellings with a continuous front replaced the earlier detached houses. A comparison of the historically valuable topographical drawings made by Whitefield in 1852 with photographs of the middle 1860's discloses the bewildering changes. In the Whitefield drawings, St. Patrick's Church and St. Mary's College stand in virtual isolation on Dorchester Street. To the west is a large open space, then the Roman Catholic cemetery, today part of Dominion Square. St. Catherine has only two houses between University and Peel. Sherbrooke Street is a country road with James McGill's old summer house on one side and his new university on the other. What a contrast photographs taken in the next decade reveal! Dorchester and St. Catherine streets are lined with continuous rows of houses; terraces and occasional detached houses appear on Sherbrooke Street.

THE
PREVAILING
MOOD

The mood, that of conciliation, is more difficult to trace, since it left no churches nor streets, and could not be captured pictorially. Perhaps the earliest clear expression of it came in 1855. The news of the storming of Sebastopol by combined French and British forces brought Montrealers into the streets, for once all on the same side. This was sensational, because, since 1849, street fighting was too often their normal form of intercourse. As recently as 1853, Montreal Protestants had encouraged the visit of the Reverend Alessandro Gavazzi, a former Roman Catholic clergyman, whose stock-in-trade was bitter denunciation of the Roman Catholic Church. Gavazzi's lecture, delivered in Zion Congregational Church, half-way up Beaver Hall Hill, ended in a riot. The Montreal police, numbering only fifty men, were entirely inadequate, and the military, when called upon, fired indiscriminately into the crowd. Yet in October 1855, Montrealers were united in their celebration. The bells of Notre Dame Church and the Anglican cathedral rang in the good news. Patriotic slogans were lit up by gas flares. Volunteer firemen, the shock troops of that age, discharged nothing more lethal than roman candles. The striking thing is that the mood lasted. In 1860, the Prince of Wales was rapturously received. Thus was ushered in the era of goodwill that extended to and beyond Confederation.

The forces that produced this welcome change in civic behaviour were many. Improved material conditions were certainly one. Good understanding among public men played a part as well. The alliance between the French and English political leaders, Cartier and

Galt, rested on more than convenience. Conciliation was preached by one section of the Montreal press. The new line began with the acquisition of *The Gazette* by Brown Chamberlain in 1853. For the next seventeen years, that is to say, until Chamberlain left Montreal, *The Gazette* was tireless in extolling the virtues of civic harmony. *La Minerve* followed the same positive line. It is probable that the two newspapers reflected the views of the business classes, French and English, and, therefore, that the desire for harmonious relations was felt on both sides. This is the period, also, in which the national societies became charitable agencies, largely losing their former political significance. In order to take better care of the needy, the St. Patrick's Society divided in 1856 into two groups, the Protestant branch taking the new name, the Irish Protestant Benevolent Society. This division clearly indicated the slackening of the national concept and the rise of the philanthropic.

A
NEIGHBOUR'S
WAR

I n the late autumn of 1860, Montrealers became absorbed in the crucial election in the United States— the one that was to bring Abraham Lincoln to the presidency. The threat of the southern states to leave the union was denounced as "mere election ruses, and . . . not to be taken into serious account." [3] Yet secession took place, and in April 1861 the Civil War, so long dreaded, began. That the Civil War was a force in the Confederation age, Montrealers were acutely aware.

Montreal was well informed upon the tensions that produced the Civil War. It was a staging-point on the secret routes across Maine or along Lake Champlain, which brought Negroes from bondage in the United States to freedom in Canada.[4] Montrealers, for example the Reverend William Bennett Bond, rector of St. George's and future Anglican archbishop, and D. P. Janes, a member of the American Presbyterian Church, were active in rescue work. Janes, indeed, was nick-named "the African consul," because of his connection with the underground railroad. The execution of John Brown, following the raid on Harper's Ferry in the autumn of 1859, produced an outburst of indignation. On December 4, there was a meeting on Victoria Square, where money was collected for the family of "the martyred Captain Brown." At the same meeting, a Montreal Anti-Slavery Society was formed.

A literary relationship between Montreal and anti-slavery was provided by *Uncle Tom's Cabin.* Harriet Beecher Stowe, a frequent visitor to Montreal, made it the happy spot where Liza found sanctuary after her many adventures. Montrealers were quick to appreciate the honour done them. The first review of Mrs. Stowe's novel to be published in Canada appeared in *The Gazette* on April 17, 1852. Later in 1852, Dawson, the Montreal publisher, brought out a Canadian edition. A French edition followed. Sir Wilfrid Laurier credited his lifelong detestation of slavery to this novel, which he read as a law student at McGill University.

Montreal sentiment favoured the northern cause throughout the four years of war. There was consider-able enlistment in the Union armies. Casualty lists that contained Montreal names appeared in the newspapers following every major battle. Six months after Fred-ericksburg (December 1862), *La Minerve* carried the names of French Canadians killed in that sanguinary engagement. At about the same time, the United States Consul wrote: "There are said to be some five hundred soldiers in the army of the United States from this city. Their wives, sisters, and mothers wish to know where they are, whether living or dead. They cannot read or write and are destitute of the means to pay postage. From reasons of humanity I have written for them to officers in command of companies and regiments."

In spite of its support of the North, the city became something of a Confederate refugee centre. For a decade or so before the Civil War, southern families had made pilgrimages to Montreal to escape the summer heat or the periodic ravages of yellow fever. The war increased the movement. Refugee civilians were joined by prisoners of war escaped from northern camps. Agents of the Confederate government visited Montreal, usually en route to Europe. In the autumn of 1864, the southerners provided Montreal with its most perilous war experience. It was from Montreal that they organized the raid on St. Albans, Vermont, and it was to Montreal that they were brought back after their capture. Neither the raid nor the local magistrate's dismissal of the raiders reflected very much credit on Montreal, in view of its professed northern sympathies.

The city may have had a close connection with the final tragedy of the Civil War, the assassination of Abraham Lincoln. John Wilkes Booth, Lincoln's murderer, was well known to Montreal theatre-goers. In the autumn of 1864, Booth was in Montreal, probably seeking a theatrical engagement, although the coincidence of his visit and the St. Albans raid is striking. He talked wildly: "Old Abe's contract was near up [the reference was to the approaching presidential election] and whether elected or not, he would get his goose cooked." Booth was rumoured to be in Montreal again in April 1865 on the eve of the assassination.

The news of the assassination of Lincoln reached Montreal on April 15, less than twelve hours after the event. "There was the greatest consternation and horror. . . . It made excitement which almost suspended business and made men look blank with amazement." The city council passed a unanimous resolution deploring the assassination and declaring April 19 an official day of mourning. The Montreal services were set to begin at noon, in order to coincide with the great memorial in Washington. One of the services was held in the American Presbyterian Church, which in those days stood on Victoria Square. The other took place in the Mechanics' Institute on St. James Street. There were numerous addresses, perhaps the most effective being delivered by Thomas D'Arcy McGee, who three years later was to fall to an assassin. At a later time public bodies carried resolutions of sympathy for the United States. The Institut canadien sent a formal address to the United States consul, denouncing "the detestable crime" and extending its sympathy to the bereaved family. This was the only Montreal group which appeared to remember that Abraham Lincoln left a wife and children.[5]

How did Montreal's wartime experience compare with that of other parts of British America? In the material sense, the impact upon Montreal was far less. It was too distant to be affected as was Toronto, Saint John, or Halifax. These three had a veritable boom in business, for they were able to provide supplies close at hand. Furthermore, Montreal's manufactures had to surmount the steep United States war tariffs, while Canada West (Ontario) and the Maritimes had free entry for the produce of their farms and fisheries.

The Civil War seems to have strengthened the resolution of those Montrealers who were intent on securing provincial union. McGee, for example, undertook a lecture tour in which he linked the enemies of union in Canada with the friends of slavery. The implication was hardly fair to the Canadian critics of Confederation, but it was powerful. There was also the stimulus of immediate experience. The Quebec Conference was in full discussion when the news of the St. Albans raid broke. In December 1864, the United States gave formal notice of its intention to terminate the Reciprocity Treaty. These events, threatening security and prosperity alike, pointed to one end: "What should be done?" asked the Montreal Corn Exchange in its third annual report, October 1865. "The immediate duty of the Governments of the . . . Provinces clearly is . . . to . . . promote commercial [and political] relations among their own people."

6 MONTREAL AND CONFEDERATION

The first Dominion Day was heralded by the crash of artillery salutes. At sunrise, the Montreal Field Battery fired from the reservoir below Pine Avenue. An hour or so later, the salute was repeated by warships lying in the river. Soon the narrow streets of the old city were bright with the light summer clothing of townsfolk and the brilliant uniforms of marching men—the scarlet of the infantry, the blue of the cavalry, and the green of the riflemen. The sun, mindful of its obligations to such an important part of the British Empire, shone splendidly. A light breeze "flaunted the broad Union Jack from the public and many private buildings," and dispelled the dust along the country roads that led from the city to Parc LaFontaine.

There, the first of the four official ceremonies marking Confederation was held. Troops—Montreal volunteer units, such as the Chasseurs canadiens, the Guides, and the Grand Trunk Battalion, as well as British regulars—formed three sides of a huge square. "The fourth [was] a dense mass of struggling spectators." Promptly at ten o'clock, carriages bearing the city council, the mayor's drawn by four white horses, wheeled into the centre of the square. The trumpeters of the hussar escort sounded a fanfare; the mayor, Henry Starnes, delivered a becoming address in French and English and then read the Queen's proclamation that called Canada into being. There were more artillery salutes, diversified by *feux de joie* fired by the infantry, the rendering of "God Save the Queen" by massed bands, and, still audible in the general din, cheers from the populace.

The council and mayor, with their mounted escort, then proceeded to other parts of the city, where the ceremony, with differences in decorative detail and volume of noise, was repeated—at Place Viger, Place d'Armes, and Victoria Square. On Place d'Armes there was an especially brilliant display. The guard of honour was mounted by the 100th Royal Canadian Regiment, the first Canadian unit ever to go overseas. It had been brought home from its garrison duties in Britain and Malta to add lustre to the first Dominion Day. Every man wore a maple leaf in his shako, and a circle of maple leaves, like a victor's crown, was carried on the staff of the regimental colours. On Victoria Square, a pleasing variation was introduced. At the conclusion of the ceremony, the fountain sprang into life, "sending a massive crystal column of water" fully as high as the five storeys of nearby Bonaventure Hall, one of the loftiest buildings in Montreal.

Festivities of a more domestic nature followed: The St. Patrick's Society sponsored a "pic-nic" at Boucherville, timed, however, so as not to clash with the official celebrations. Small steamers took parties of holidaymakers to Carillon on the Ottawa River. In the afternoon, a lacrosse match was played on the cricket grounds beside St. James the Apostle's church. The contenders were a Montreal team and the Caughnawaga Indians; as was appropriate, the Indians won. Nor was the cultural aspect neglected. A poet produced an ode to Dominion Day in fourteen sections and thirty-one verses.

Darkness brought the grand climax. This took the form of firework displays near the reservoir and on Place Viger. Neither time nor expense was spared. An emissary secured in Boston "pieces . . . even new in the firework-loving land of the Fourth of July." They consisted of "devices and mottoes": "The Nation's Birthday"; "The Crown, VR"; "The Ocean Ferry" (a steamship in motion); "Vive la Confédération" (a masterpiece in which joined hands, provincial coats of arms, and mottoes were all mingled). At nine o'clock the firing of "floral shells" announced the beginning of the last spectacle. The fireworks continued well into the summer night and were echoed by minor displays in neighbouring towns. St. Lambert lit up two enormous bonfires on Moffatt's Island (now swallowed in the Seaway embankment). Montrealers must have felt amply compensated for loss of sleep and the expenditure of $1,000 in their expectation of "the new epoch . . . in the . . . history . . . of mankind" ushered in by Confederation.[1]

MONTREAL'S FATHERS OF CONFEDERATION

The long and checkered struggle that underlay the union of the British American provinces is well known. Less well known is Montreal's part. Montreal had two interests at stake: it wanted escape from the political shortcomings of the Act of Union, which had united Lower and Upper Canada in 1840, and a more complete realization of the economic advantages that the Act had promised.

Placed as Montreal was, midway between an overwhelmingly French-Canadian east (the former Lower Canada) and an equally overwhelmingly Anglo-Canadian west (the former Upper Canada), it saw all too clearly the impossibility of containing two races in a single constitutional frame such as the Province of Canada. It had only to recollect the racial overtones of the riots and the burning of the Parliament House in 1849.

The Act of Union had contributed to Montreal's economic well-being. In combining the resources of the two old provinces, the Act had made possible the paraphernalia of canals and railways, the sinews of Montreal business. In 1857 there was an onset of hard times. They originated in overspeculation and bank failure in the United States midwest. The effects were felt first in New York, then in London, and finally in Canada. Since the depression was more acute in Canada West than in Canada East, the Province was again divided in outlook, this time on an economic basis. A comment by the Montreal Board of Trade is revealing: "Canada felt the full force of the blow, the west especially. In Montreal, the Bank of Montreal stood like a rock. . . . [It] enabled the city largely to escape the effects of this terrible shock."

Solutions for the impasse (political and economic) were advanced by a number of public men, Montrealers or in some way connected with Montreal interests. In 1856, the year before the business collapse, Antoine

Aimé Dorion, a lawyer and one of the Montreal members of parliament, had suggested federalizing the two parts of the Province of Canada in order to reduce political tension. His proposal was made as an amendment to a motion by William Lyon Mackenzie calling for the dissolution of the Union. Dorion acted with the approval of his political friends in parliament, one of whom, Alexander Tilloch Galt, was, two years later, to carry the federal proposal very much further. Meanwhile, in March 1858, Alexander Morris delivered in Montreal an important address, in which he urged the federalizing of all the British American provinces and the addition of the Hudson's Bay Company's territories and British Columbia. The latter were areas generally outside the thinking of Canadians. The address was later published and given wide circulation under the title *Nova Britannia*. Morris, McGill's first graduate in Arts, and one of its first graduating class in Law, entered parliament in 1861, as member for Lanark South. In about the same period (1856-58) Thomas D'Arcy McGee, the brilliant orator and author, adopted the cause of general federation. At first the champion of the Irish, McGee now sought to merge French, Scots, English, and Irish, to form "a new nationality." Provincial union was a means of extending his concept to include all of British North America. His position was greatly strengthened by his election to parliament in 1857 as a member for Montreal.

In the late summer of 1858, A. T. Galt, mentioned above as an ally of Dorion's, was invited to enter the cabinet. Galt sat for Sherbrooke, but his banking and railway interests drew him increasingly to Montreal. He entered only on condition that the cabinet accept the objective of general federation and the acquisition of the western territories. George-Etienne Cartier, a member for Montreal and joint Prime Minister (with John A. Macdonald of Canada West), then made Galt's plan part of his legislative program. (Canada at that time had two joint prime ministers, one representing the eastern, the other the western, part of the Province. The one who had the larger following—in this instance Cartier—was considered to be the "first," or senior, prime minister.)

The proposed constitutional framework of a central government and provincial governments would permit full exercise of local tendencies, yet could secure common action in interests common to all. An economic framework would make the resources of all the federation available for what Cartier was fond of calling "great enterprises of national interest." Specifically, a free trade area, extending from the Atlantic to the head of the Great Lakes (the practical limits of British America at that time), would be created. Of this region, nature had made Montreal the geographical centre; Confederation would make it the business centre as well.

Dorion, who had originated the idea of federation within the Province of Canada, now refused to accept the federation of all the provinces; he became, indeed, the proposal's most determined opponent. Cartier found little support for general federation outside his own province. For the moment at any rate, he put the proposition aside. In 1863 and 1864, however, as a result of the increasing tensions of the Civil War, the subject of provincial union became, for Montrealers, urgent. It passed from an interest of the few to the vital concern of all.

THE COMMON
MAN AND
CONFEDERATION

How did the common man show his concern? There is no very complete evidence. The newspapers form a poor index. They were biased by their political allegiance. *La Minerve* and *The Gazette* were the mouthpiece of George-Etienne Cartier, who at this point (1864) revived his union interests and became the main Montreal driving force towards Confederation. Diary entries and personal letters are more revealing of individual attitudes. Covering the Confederation period was the diary of George Edward Clerk.[2] As a Scot, he could view Montreal with a degree of detachment; married to a French Canadian, he entered fully into the hopes and fears of her people. Clerk was the proprietor and editor of the *True Witness,* a newspaper that he wished to make the voice of conservative Roman Catholic views. His first references to provincial union were made in June and July 1864, when he was painfully shocked by "the unnatural alliance" of the Upper Canada reformer George Brown and George-Etienne Cartier. Disagreeing on almost everything else, they suddenly agreed on the necessity of Confederation, with dire consequences, Clerk feared. On December 31, 1864, he wrote: "In Canada the year will be remarkable as having . . . in June the disgraceful coalition of Brown and Cartier and a system of union, mis-called Confederation. . . . This scheme . . . will ruin French nationality and menace all our peculiar religious institutions." Clerk was a disapproving recorder of the first Dominion Day: "July 1. Monday . . . today was kept as a holiday on which the Union act came into force. George and Charlie went to a picnic on Nuns' Island. In the forenoon, turn-out of troops. In the evening, fireworks: No great thing."

A more comprehensive summary of opinion was provided by W. J. Dawson, the principal of McGill University. Writing in 1866 to his friend and fellow Nova Scotian, Joseph Howe, he said: "I suppose scarcely any one among the English of Lower Canada desires Confederation . . . but many would like to have a legislative union. Among the French, nearly one-half are against the Scheme. The English in general take a very despondent view, feeling themselves politically powerless." [3] A more courageous note was entered by the Reverend Henry Wilkes, the Montreal Congregational minister, who recalled "a patriotic celebration" on board SS *Moravian,* where he was overtaken by the first Dominion Day while at sea. [4]

Political events of 1865 and 1867 throw a good deal of light on Montreal attitudes towards Confederation. In 1865, the so-called Confederation debates took place in the Canadian parliament. The three Montreal members, Cartier of Montreal East, John Rose of Montreal Centre, and D'Arcy McGee of Montreal West, all voted to approve the Seventy-two Resolutions of the Quebec Conference—in other words, in favour of Confederation. Whether their constituents would have supported them cannot be known, since there was no general election. Two years later, however, the first elections for the Canadian federal parliament and for the Quebec legislature were held. If there was resentment, here was a chance to ventilate it. "The friends of union," however, were successful. Cartier, the chief Montreal architect of Confederation, was returned for both houses, the "double mandate" that was then in force making this possible. If they had wished to do so, his constituents in Montreal East could have defeated him. McGee, whose adherence to Confederation was quite as forthright as Cartier's, was returned in Montreal West, and the pro-Confederation Thomas Workman in Montreal Centre. To the Quebec parliament, along with Cartier, Edward Carter and Alexander Ogilvie, both friends of Confederation, were elected.[5] There could be no reasonable doubt about the direction in which Montreal sentiment lay.

THE CRITICS
OF
CONFEDERATION

Along with the doubting Thomases were outright opponents of Confederation. In first rank was Antoine Aimé Dorion. His attacks, whether in the parliamentary debates of 1865 or in the elections to the first federal parliament in 1867, were consistent. (He was returned in 1867 for the County of Hochelaga, which he had represented from 1861.) Dorion feared for French-Canadian survival. Unfortunately for the effectiveness of his appeal, he allowed other issues to intrude—for example, the undue influence exercised by the great banks and railways. Furthermore, Dorion had the liability of some very odd allies. Médéric Lanctôt and Laurent-Olivier David were so extreme in their views that they laid themselves open to charges of radicalism and annexationism. (Both men had careers of significance in later Montreal history: Lanctôt as a workingman's leader; David, as a *littérateur* and civic official.) Their extravagance played directly into Cartier's hands, enabling him to denounce the conscientious critics along with "le parti canadien-francais extrême et le parti annexationiste ou américain." Of the French and Anglo-Canadians who feared for their particular community, Cartier made sport. He called them "messieurs qui ont peur, les uns les autres." Cartier made his appeal to all men of goodwill: "La population francaise en confiant ses intérêts à un gouvernement fédéral a preuve de confiance en nos compatriotes anglais. Est-ce trop de demander à la race anglaise qu'elle se fie à la liberté et l'esprit de justice de la race francaise dans le gouvernement local?" [6]

AN
OPPORTUNITY
MISSED

The critics of Confederation failed to score an obvious point, when the resolutions of the Quebec Conference were debated in 1865. Dorion, who feared Anglo-Canadian domination outside Quebec, and Christopher Dunkin, who feared French-Canadian domination inside Quebec, overlooked an interest they had in common, in their anxiety to advance those they had in particular. The autonomy of Montreal, and of other towns and cities, was a concern of all, yet it was espoused by none. "Municipal institutions," not a very precise term, were relegated to provincial jurisdiction in Section XCII of the British North America Act. The municipalities were made subject to the provinces. This was a strange reversal of nearly thirty years of Canadian experience: the Durham *Report on the Affairs of British North America,* distilling the wisdom of English reformers, had placed effective municipal government high in the priorities of its recommendations. In fact, it was one of the earliest of the recommendations to be put into effect. When Lord Sydenham, Durham's successor, who did not get round to responsible government at all, granted Montreal a charter in August 1840, he gave the city much wider powers than those assigned by the charter of 1833. In 1849, Baldwin and

LaFontaine, the winners of responsible government, were authors of the Municipal Corporations Act, a measure that extended self-government to the countryside. Confederation, however, halted this forward march. The Province of Quebec became Montreal's master. It was not a harsh master, but it had many duties, and the attention it gave Montreal was intermittent. The limited powers the city possessed were never sufficient for its needs. It was under-represented in the provincial legislature; hence, it could not easily draw attention to its plight.

THE
DEBIT SIDE OF
THE LEDGER

Confederation was not all gain for Montreal. Its political hopes were finally dashed, when Ottawa became the capital of the Dominion, and Quebec that of the Province. (Hope—more wishful thinking than conviction—was not entirely without foundation: as recently as 1861, the Diocese of Montreal had been designated as the Metropolitan See for the Anglican Ecclesiastical Province of Canada.) Failure to be chosen was not simply a wound to pride. Montreal lost to Quebec the fine library that the Department of Education had built up. Education, like certain other departments, had remained seated in Montreal, although the capital before Confederation had alternated between Toronto and Quebec, following Montreal's loss of its capital position in 1849 (see Chapter 3). Now any ambitious Montrealers who aspired to civil service posts had to leave their native city, and they left it the poorer.

Montreal might take pride in its commercial pre-eminence. Even this, however, was qualified. Toronto was a clearly defined rival. Confederation confirmed its character as a provincial capital and did nothing to diminish the substantial economic position it occupied. In the immediate Confederation period, Montreal tried, and failed, to assert financial control over Toronto. The collapse of the Bank of Upper Canada (1866) and the failure of the Commercial Bank (1867)—both Toronto institutions—were gains for Montreal. But other Toronto banks remained firm, and so Toronto's financial independence was secured. This boded ill for Montrealers, who sought to compensate for their political sacrifices by economic gains.

7 ACROSS THE CONTINENT AND BEYOND

Confederation brought enormous advantages to the port of Montreal through federally made improvements outside the port. The Lachine Canal, which had been enlarged in the 1840's, was enlarged again in the 1870's. In the view of the gentlemen of the Corn Exchange, this made it even more "the artery of commerce." The phrase may seem inflated, but it underscores the importance to Montreal of trade from the west. Of equal importance was the route to the east. The river channel to Quebec was of vital concern, as were also the navigational problems of the river east of Quebec. The new federal government assumed responsibility for river service: channel marking, lighthouses, dredging, and so on. The consequences were very great. By 1880 the Allan Line doubled its fleet and more than doubled its tonnage. It adopted as its house flag a copy of the French tricolour, a reminder, into whatever port its ships sailed, of Canada's dual tradition. Between 1870 and 1880, two additional ocean lines (the Dominion and the Beaver, from the British Isles) made Montreal a regular port of call.

Confederation also brought to Montreal a revival of interest in railways. The old desire to escape from dependence upon the Grand Trunk was still present. Also present was the new idea of opening communication by rail with the north and the far west. The success of the United States in the construction of its first transcontinental railway system (1869) was not lost on Montreal. The acquisition by Canada (1869) of the territories of the Hudson's Bay Company opened an opportunity, especially in the view of such expansionists as Sir George-Etienne Cartier. Sir Hugh Allan (as he became in 1871) lent his weight. Another persuasive figure appeared—this one altruistic in his motives. He was the Reverend Antoine Labelle, the *curé* of St. Jerome. This young priest, popularly known as "le roi du nord," was obsessed with the idea of a railway to open the Laurentians.

THE QUEBEC MONTREAL OTTAWA AND OCCIDENTAL

Father Labelle's aim was to colonize the mountain country beyond St. Jerome and provide farm homes for the increasing population of Montreal. In 1872 and again in 1876, Labelle showed the benefits that Montreal might derive, when he and his parishioners brought south one hundred sleigh loads of cord wood for the Montreal poor. Promotion of this kind was irresistible; the Montreal City Council voted one million dollars to assist the Northern Colonization Railway project. However, the plan was greatly modified and Labelle's purpose defeated. The St. Jerome line was extended west to Ottawa instead of north, as Labelle had wished. A line from Quebec was built to meet the Ottawa–St. Jerome–Montreal line at St. Martin's Junction, just north of Montreal. The official title of this railway, commonly called the North Shore, was the Quebec Montreal Ottawa and Occidental (QMO&O). The traditional silver spike was driven at Terrebonne, February 1878, by Mme Joly, the wife of the Premier of Quebec.

The new railway made important changes in Montreal. Its shops, marshalling yards, and principal passenger station were in what was then the eastern part of the city. The North Shore Railway imparted to eastern Montreal something of the impetus that the Grand Trunk had given to the west. But for Montreal as a whole the outcome was a disappointment. It failed to find in Ottawa the rich source of revenue it had expected. Furthermore, Quebec, not itself, was in the advantageous position of being the deep-water terminus of the new railway.

THE
TRANSCONTINENTAL
—FAILURE

The first transcontinental railway project grew out of Confederation. To Sir George-Etienne Cartier, it was a means of achieving one of the ends of Confederation. In his view, the union of the eastern provinces had been the prerequisite for gaining possession of the West. The West would provide living space for eastern Canada and would provide also the stage on which French and English Canadians would work out their destiny of co-operation. These concepts, partly material, partly mystic, account for Cartier's activity in stirring up interest in western projects. Confederation of the four eastern provinces was followed by the purchase of Rupert's Land (the territory of the Hudson's Bay Company) in 1869.[1] He was the chief figure, on the government side, both in the negotiation for the purchase of Rupert's Land and in the planning of the railway.[2] Sir Hugh Allan was deeply concerned as well. The railway recommended itself to him as the means of reaching beyond Montreal, the western terminus of his shipping line. Both Cartier and Allan regarded Montreal as the key to their western ambitions. Unfortunately, the two men disagreed about whose hand should be on the key.

Cartier was bound to the Grand Trunk Railway by material and political interests. He had been the Company's solicitor from its incorporation and held a considerable amount of Grand Trunk stock. The Grand Trunk was interested in securing the charter, and Cartier's political life was bound up in the opportunity for patronage that the Railway gave him. The Grand Trunk had an important advantage as a transcontinental railway builder. It was already about half-way to transcontinental proportions: in the east, it went as far as Rivière du Loup, where it made connection with the federally owned railway (the Intercolonial, completed in 1876) that extended to Halifax; in the west, it reached Chicago, via Sarnia.

Allan did not share Cartier's preference for the Grand Trunk as the builder of the transcontinental. He seems to have had the distaste generally felt by Montreal businessmen for the Grand Trunk. Moreover, he had interests in eastern Montreal and on the north shore of the Ottawa River. These, he knew, could be better served by a railway under his own control—not under the Grand Trunk's.[3] Thus Cartier and Allan tended to neutralize each other. The Grand Trunk finally withdrew from the competition, discouraged by some of the restrictions laid down by the Canadian government, but Allan had other competitors. He improved his position by taking up the North Shore Railway scheme, described earlier in the chapter, and by the promise that it would be used to develop eastern Montreal. Allan was temporarily successful. In the federal election of 1872, he conspired to bring about the defeat of Cartier in Montreal East. At the same time, he advanced substantial sums of money to the Conservative leaders, Cartier included, for election purposes. Early in 1873, Allan was awarded the railway contract—in return, it was later alleged, for his contributions to Conservative campaign funds. The allegations formed the basis of the Pacific Scandal, which broke in the late summer of 1873. Allan had won an empty victory: the charter was taken away. Before the scandal broke, Cartier was dead.

Such was the damaging—indeed, tragic—connection of Montreal with the first plan for a transcontinental railway. The city and city interests had been deeply involved, from the hopeful beginning to the sordid conclusion. It was a Montreal newspaper, the *Herald,* that published the incriminating correspondence between Allan and the Conservative government leaders.

FRUSTRATION

A long pause followed: Montreal was distracted, first by the depressed conditions of the middle 1870's and next by the outbreak of racial and religious strife. The old leaders, such as Allan, were discredited. The necessity for a railway did not diminish, but the means, and perhaps also the heart, were lacking. It was not till towards the end of the gloomy 1870's that there was a revival of interest. The federal election of 1878, with its Conservative victory (in which Montreal shared to the extent of all three seats), brought the National Policy and, with the National Policy, hope for the transcontinental railway.

In the early 1870's, there had been an informal truce between the Grand Trunk and Montreal. The railway extended its tracks to the wharves (1871), and the city constructed bridges for it across the Lachine Canal. But the hard times that followed 1873 brought back the feud. Grand Trunk rates continued to be discriminatory. To make matters worse, the Grand Trunk absorbed local railways that Montreal had hoped would become effective rivals. These were the railways built originally to St. Jean and Lachine and later much extended. The building of new railways on the south shore of the St. Lawrence in 1873 and 1880 provided no relief. It was alleged that the Grand Trunk hindered their financing through its influence in the English money market. Be this as it may, it rendered them ineffective by denying them the use of the Victoria Bridge. A second bridge to break this blockade was projected across the lower end of St. Helen's Island, on much the same site as that of the present Jacques Cartier Bridge. It was never built, but a name was assigned, a dignified retort —the Royal Albert. For a few summers, the rival railways used the prosaic expedient of a ferry; in the winter, the anything-but-prosaic expedient of an ice railway. Track was laid on the ice of the St. Lawrence during four successive winters, 1879-80, 1880-81, 1881-82, and 1882-83, and the trains were moved by horses or by small locomotives. In January of 1881, one of the engines fell through the ice, or as an official explained it with great presence of mind, 'la locomotive est arrêtée ici pour prendre l'eau.' [4]

The cold douche was symbolic—both of the rival railways' failure and of Montreal's hopelessness of attaining a commanding position in transportation in eastern America. As the attractions of the far west grew, Montreal's expectations in the east diminished. Therefore, there was engendered the frame of mind that would applaud the project of a transcontinental railway built by Montrealers and based on Montreal.

THE TRANSCONTINENTAL —SUCCESS

Three Montrealers made the railway real. In popular esteem at any rate, the first was Lord Strathcona.[5] Donald Smith, as he had come from Scotland, had had a fleeting acquaintance with Montreal in the 1830's. Then in 1838, at the age of eighteen, he had vanished into the wilds of northeastern Labrador as a servant of the Hudson's Bay Company. He reappeared in Montreal in the Confederation era, when his ability to place considerable investments (he acted as the agent for numerous Hudson's Bay employees) enabled him to cut a figure in banking circles. In 1869, the Hudson's Bay Company made him manager of the Montreal district. He had none of the prejudices of the fur-trading west against agricultural settlement. His instincts were those of a land speculator, and these, doubtless, had been sharpened by early successes in Montreal real estate. He became a national figure in 1870, when he offered a pacific solution for the Manitoba rebellion. By 1873 or 1874, his interests had crystallized. He took charge of land sales for the Hudson's Bay Company. (The Company had retained one twentieth of the land in the fertile belt.) Land sales were impossible without settlers, and settlers were hard to get without a railway.

Smith had been a member of the original transcontinental railway group in 1872 and 1873. Following the collapse of that venture, he turned towards local railways in the west, especially the St. Paul, Minneapolis and Manitoba, more briefly known as the Red River Valley Railway. He interested others in western railways, notably his cousin George Stephen, then the president of the Bank of Montreal, and later the first president of the Canadian Pacific Railway, when it was

51

formed in 1881.[6] Smith did not become a director of the Canadian Pacific Railway Company immediately, although he subscribed to the purchase of five thousand shares of its stock, the same amount held by the president and by the vice-president. His experience in land development and settlement made him a valuable ally. In 1882, he became a director, and his growing importance was symbolized when he drove the last spike (characteristically, Smith chose a common utilitarian iron one) in November 1885 at Craighellachie in British Columbia.

By this time Smith was completely identified with Montreal. He had long since become a property owner. The various houses he occupied in Montreal form a nice index of his rise in the city. His first house was on University Street, a substantial, but hardly grand, neighbourhood. Later he moved to another terraced house, this time on Mansfield not far from Dorchester Street, a site now covered by Place Ville Marie. Finally, he achieved red stone splendour on Dorchester itself. This mansion, at the corner of Fort Street, has long since disappeared, but fragments of it—the stained glass windows that decorated its dining room—are preserved in the Royal Victoria College of McGill University. In 1886, he was elected to the federal parliament as a member for Montreal and was knighted. When, eleven years later (1897), he was raised to the peerage, part of the title he chose honoured the city whose fortunes were so much his own: he became Lord Strathcona and Mount Royal.

An even more authentically Montreal figure was George Stephen. His contacts with the city began in 1850, and he became a permanent resident about five years later. Stephen was first an importer of woollens and cottons; later, a manufacturer. He became interested in banking, in both its practical and theoretical aspects. It was in the capacity of the practical banker that he channelled Donald Smith's investments to the Bank of Montreal, of which he (Stephen) was successively director and president. Stephen's interest in the theoretical aspects of banking may have been simply another evidence of his intense intellectual curiosity. He was, for example, greatly concerned with oriental studies. Doubtless, by his Montreal contemporaries, these were looked upon as harmless entertainment; yet they were destined, many years later, to have a very practical application, in encouraging the company to develop trans-Pacific trade. In the late 1870's Stephen was drawn into western railway speculation, probably by Donald Smith. The venture in the Red River Valley Railway was most profitable. Indeed, it is said to have earned Stephen a second fortune, making him, by a comfortable margin, the richest man in Montreal. Be this as it may, Stephen's successes in Manitoba disposed him to the greater opportunities of the transcontinental railway.

Sir John A. Macdonald, the Prime Minister, was anxious to revive the transcontinental plan and only wanted men to finance it. Said a friend regarding Stephen and his Red River Railway associates: "Get their money for your . . . Pacific [project] before they have time to invest it somewhere else." Stephen and Macdonald were on intimate terms, and conversations between them on the subject of the railway began in 1880. By 1881 Stephen had found the capitalists and the practical railway men who were to work with him. It was this group, known as the Canadian Pacific Railway Company, that received the contract to build the transcontinental, with government aid, from "a point on Lake Nipissing [in northeastern Ontario] to the Pacific." (It was not the intention of the government to assume responsibility east of Lake Nipissing, since to do so might favour one city more than another. The building of the rail line to Toronto or Montreal would, in either case, be left to civic initiative.)

In February 1881, Stephen became the first president of the Canadian Pacific Railway. Merchant, manufacturer, banker, railway-builder, Stephen reflected perfectly the four great economic trends of post-Confederation Montreal. In 1888, he was raised to the peerage as Lord Mount Stephen, the first Canadian to be so honoured. There is a fine statue of Stephen in the Windsor Station. His true memorial is the Royal Victoria Hospital, of which he was one of the principal inspirations and donors.

The third Montrealer of the triumvirate was introduced through Stephen. He was R. B. Angus. The two men were associated in the Bank of Montreal; Angus was manager and Stephen president. Angus had extensive knowledge of the United States, having held Bank of Montreal managerial posts there, first in Chicago and then in New York. Probably few Montrealers knew the vital northwestern area of the United States better than he. Angus was the confidant of both Smith and Stephen. The triumvirate was very tightly knit. It was also closely attached to Montreal.

THE
CANADIAN PACIFIC
IN MONTREAL

Probably the Smith-Stephen-Angus triumvirate would have been sufficient to make Montreal the headquarters of the new railway, but a fourth person smoothed their way. He was Duncan McIntyre, the controlling force in many railways, actual or projected. Two were of the greatest importance to Montreal. The first (already in existence) was the line between Callendar, on Lake Nipissing (designated as the eastern terminus of the transcontinental Canadian Pacific), and Ottawa. The second (still to be built) was the line between Ottawa and the Atlantic coast, by way of Montreal. The Ottawa-Montreal line was to follow the south shore of the Ottawa River. It was to bridge the St. Lawrence at Montreal and in this way to deal a blow to the Grand Trunk's monopoly. Stephen had a financial interest in this venture of McIntyre's. McIntyre became Stephen's vice-president in the Canadian Pacific. Thus, the fortunes of his railways were linked with those of the transcontinental, and Montreal's place in the general system clinched.

The material consequences of the new railway were rapidly felt. The Canadian Pacific was first brought into Montreal through the purchase of the Montreal-Ottawa section of the North Shore Railway (QMO&O). This acquisition gave the Canadian Pacific a passenger station, freight marshalling yards, and shops, all in the eastern end of Montreal. Surely the ghosts of many earlier quarrels were quieted when from the Dalhousie Station, as the eastern terminus was called, the first transcontinental train steamed away (June 28, 1886). The spirit of the future was propitiated, too, since two of the cars of the train were named *Honolulu* and *Yokohama.*

Inevitably, Montreal deployed the Canadian Pacific against the Grand Trunk. It is a fair supposition that it was as a means of breaking the old monopoly that the new railway was most widely appreciated. One monopoly belonged by right of ownership to the Grand Trunk—the only existing means of crossing the St. Lawrence. At first the rivals compromised: the Canadian Pacific used the Victoria Bridge and the Bonaventure Station in western Montreal on a rental basis. However, the service to the south had no physical connection with the lines to the north and west. The Canadian Pacific had to reach warm water, "Montreal being," as Stephen ruefully observed, "only a six-months port." In July 1887 the Canadian Pacific provided itself with its own river-crossing in a bridge at Lachine. The Lachine bridge made the Canadian Pacific independent. It made Montreal independent also.

The Lachine bridge was the key to further development. The Canadian Pacific resolved to build a western station of its own and to house in the new structure its head offices. Bruce Price, the outstanding American architect, was directed to design what was first known as the Windsor Street Station. It was officially opened in February 1887. A line ran from it to Montreal Junction (modern Montreal West), where it met one brought down from the North Shore Railway. The transcontinental then crossed the Lachine bridge, continued east, and finally touched warm water, as Stephen desired it should, at Saint John in New Brunswick.

The Lachine bridge and the Windsor Station gave the Canadian Pacific a stake in western Montreal. The Station, even in the first unit of Price's design, made an imposing adddition to the buildings surrounding Dominion Square. Beside the Station stood St. George's Church and, only a little more distant, the Dominion

Methodist Church, the ancestor of Dominion-Douglas. Across Dorchester Street was the Windsor Hotel, the most recently established and probably the most select hotel in Montreal. Diagonally across from the station was St. James Cathedral, by this time rapidly marching towards completion under the vigorous drive of Archbishop Fabre. The Windsor Station thus established the Railway's position on Dominion Square, the heart and centre of late nineteenth-century Montreal.

The hierarchy of the Railway continued to live in Montreal, and some of the members contributed richly to the city's legend. Three of the early presidents, Stephen, Smith, and Shaughnessy, were elevated to the peerage. Van Horne, the second president, was made a knight. In that imperial age, these honours were widely appreciated. Strathcona became Canadian High Commissioner to the United Kingdom, and, as such, a link between London and Montreal. Sir William Van Horne was a discriminating art collector (as well as being a talented amateur artist). He was one of the earliest to appreciate the French impressionists and the Dutch school of painters typified by Josef Israels. The great city mansions of the Railway's chief officers reared their grey or brown stone fronts on Sherbrooke and Dorchester streets. The employment of Bruce Price as the designer of Canadian Pacific buildings had considerable effect on Montreal taste. His preferred style of architecture was Romanesque, and he combined this with heavy stone work to produce a building of solidity and dignity. Price's station was only the northeast corner of the present structure, yet its design could be magnified effectively to the full proportions of the modern Windsor Station, one of the most satisfying secular buildings in Montreal.[7] Price also designed for the Bank of Montreal and for McGill University, always showing a fine sense of proportion and mass. No doubt, the new styles in architecture would have come to Montreal unaided, yet it is incontestable that their acceptance was hastened by the approval the Railway gave them.

MONTREAL
AND
THE WEST

The benefits of the new railway were felt even before the Pacific was reached. The port of Montreal began to receive cattle from eastern Ontario, lumber from the upper Ottawa, and cereals from Manitoba, all before November 1885. Reciprocally, the new western communities drew supplies and settlers from Montreal. Winnipeg (Fort Garry of the early days) became the headquarters of the new West; Regina and Calgary, hitherto Mounted Police posts, grew into cities on the line of the Railway. Sometimes it was advice they were fortified with, for example, when the Montreal Hunt, replying to a request from the Alberta Ranche, sent "the Rules of the Montreal Pack." On one note-worthy occasion, Montreal, or rather a Montrealer, named a new city. In the spring of 1884, when the virtually uninhabited Burrard Inlet was chosen as the terminus, Van Horne, then vice-president of the Rail-way, insisted that it be called Vancouver.[8]

THE NEW
NORTH-WEST
PASSAGE

Late in July 1886, there took place at the Pacific end of the new transcontinental railway an event that forecast great things for Montreal. A cargo of tea, brought by ship from Japan and consigned to the Montreal house of James Magor, was put on a train and sent eastward. A commercial route across the continent in Canadian territory was now a reality. *Punch* cele-brated the accomplishment by a drawing entitled "The New North-West Passage." The Canadian Pacific quickly capitalized on this promising start. It char-tered three vessels to provide service in the Pacific until its own three were completed in 1891. The new ships—the *Empress of India,* the *Empress of Japan,* and the *Empress of China*—were handsome vessels, clipper-bowed, with rakish funnels and masts, and wearing the Company's now well-known livery of white and buff. Montreal could at last reach not only across the continent, but across the ocean beyond.

8 O GOD!
O MONTREAL!

The Discobolus is put here because he is vulgar—
He has neither vest nor pants with which to cover
*   his limbs;*
I, Sir, am a person of most respectable connexions—
My brother-in-law is haberdasher to Mr. Spurgeon . . .

So wrote Samuel Butler in his celebrated *Psalm of Montreal,* with its devastating refrain, "O God! O Montreal!" Butler, essayist, connoisseur, and philosopher, lived in Montreal in the early 1870's. He was in despair at the contrast between the sublimity of the city's situation and the Philistinism of its inhabitants. Butler had found a splendid cast of the Discobolus hidden away, because, as the custodian said, it was vulgar. Admitting that Montreal was neither an Athens nor a Paris (some of its admirers believed more restrainedly that it might be an Edinburgh), what may be said of things of the mind and the spirit in late nineteenth-century Montreal?

Montreal was well supplied with the formal agencies that foster intellectual and artistic interests. At Confederation, it could boast one university, two classical colleges, one convent school of outstanding merit, and a range of private and public schools. A generation later, when a stock-taking might with profit be made, the outlook was even brighter. There were two universities, additional classical colleges and convents, and a much wider range of schools. Nor were informal agencies lacking—libraries, literary and artistic associations, and so forth. Finally, the newspaper press was still a constructive force not to be despised.

UNIVERSITIES

The older university, McGill, enjoyed continuity from 1829, when the Faculty of Medicine was formed. In 1872, Medicine left its old noisome quarters on Côté

Street for the Sherbrooke Street campus, where Arts and Applied Science already were. Arts had been there since its establishment in 1843, except for the period 1852 to 1860, when shortage of funds forced it to occupy the cheaper Burnside Hall, at Dorchester and University. Lectures in engineering had been given from 1855 but allowed to lapse about 1864. In 1871, the threat presented by the School of Practical Science, about to be set up in Toronto by the Ontario government, spurred McGill to create a department of Applied Science within the Faculty of Arts. The Faculty of Law, set up in 1848, held lectures in various places over the years—for example, at Burnside Hall, at Molson's Bank, and in the chambers of the Dean, who till the turn of the century was a practising lawyer.

With the move of Medicine to the Sherbrooke campus, the energies of the principal, J. W. (later Sir William) Dawson, could at last be effectively concentrated. The seventies were the middle point of his fruitful career, which began in 1855 and was to go on till his retirement in 1893. His dream was for a university where "practical results . . . suitable to Canada" might be achieved; hence his cultivation of the professional faculties of Medicine and Law and of the normal school acquired from the Anglican Church in 1857. Sustaining Dawson's efforts were the great Montreal merchant families—Molson, Workman, Redpath, McDonald. They contributed generously to endowments, scholarships, and building funds. Before the end of the century, the campus, with its broad grass sward, fine avenue of elms, and dignified buildings— Arts, Medical, Engineering, Chemistry, Physics, Library, and Museum—had much of its modern appearance.

Two matters were of deep personal concern to Dawson. The first was that students for the Christian ministry should benefit from university training. As a result of his encouragement, four theological colleges —Presbyterian, Congregational, Anglican, and Methodist—were affiliated with McGill during his principalship. Secondly, Dawson was resolved to obtain higher education for women. In 1889, the old Principal had the satisfaction of seeing the first women graduate. The Dawson era fixed the character of McGill. It was thoroughly in harmony with the Montreal of that time—practical, progressive, and fundamentally Christian. It reflected another facet of the society in which it was set: both French-speaking and English-speaking Canadians were found on the teaching staff and among the student body.

The appearance of a French-Canadian university was delayed by an extraordinary combination of circumstances and controversies. There was no lack of teaching institutions upon which to base a university: On November 1, 1840, in virtue of a "concordat" between Bishop Bourget and the Sulpicians, the latter undertook the training of clergy for the Roman Catholic Diocese of Montreal.[1] Three years later, there was established in Montreal a medical school that was initially both French-Canadian and Anglo-Canadian, but later overwhelmingly French-Canadian, in staff and students. Here were two potential faculties, but no university. The Ecole de Médecine et Chirurgie got over the difficulty in 1866 by affiliating with (and thus obtaining degrees from) Victoria University. This was an unusual alliance, since Victoria was in Ontario, and was, moreover, a Methodist foundation. From 1851 to 1867 there existed a third potential university faculty for French-speaking Roman Catholics in Montreal—a school of Law, attached to St. Mary's College.

Bishop Bourget sought a charter for a university at Montreal, only to be opposed by Laval University at Quebec (chartered in 1852), which insisted that there was room in the province for only one French-Canadian university—itself. According to the ultramontane newspaper Le Nouveau Monde, the Institut canadien too had a vision of a French university at Montreal—but one completely independent of the Church.[2] (For the fate of its dreams, see later in the chapter.) It set up courses in Law in 1866, and in 1868 affiliated itself with Victoria University. In 1871, both its staff and its students were taken into the McGill Law faculty. It was not until nine years after Confederation, in 1876, that agreement within the Church allowed for the establishment of university faculties for French-speaking Montreal—and then only as parts of a division of Laval. The

Montreal division of Laval was formally inaugurated in 1878.

The Theology and Law faculties became active in 1878; a Faculty of Arts, along with its affiliate the Ecole Polytechnique, in 1887. (The Arts faculty, like that of Law, was a new creation, but the school of engineering went back to 1873.) The Faculty of Medicine, established in 1879, encountered difficulty, since the Ecole de Médecine Victoria, already in existence, challenged the right of the new creation. The two schools were reconciled only in 1891. In 1889, Collège Sainte-Marie (St. Mary's) also was given the right to present its graduates for Laval degrees. This change in its charter had far-reaching effects upon English-speaking Roman Catholic Montreal. In 1888 St. Mary's had expanded its teaching in English to produce a complete English division; in 1899, ten years after the enlargement of the charter, the English side of St. Mary's became a separate college, Loyola, also giving its degrees through Laval.[3]

Over the years, new faculties continued to be added to the Laval division in Montreal, and at last, in 1919, the division became the autonomous Université de Montréal. Except for Loyola College, which moved a number of times and in 1916 came to its present site near Montreal West, the new university remained until the early 1940's at St. Denis and St. Catherine, where the first university building had been erected in 1893. This fine structure, with its curving outside stairway and pillared loggia, still stands, and near it is the Eglise Notre-Dame de Lourdes, which served as the university chapel.

SCHOOLS

Both universities were dependent upon good schools below them. At the secondary level, these were, until 1870 all private schools. For French-speaking Montreal, there was one with a very long history, the Collège de Montréal, founded by the Sulpicians in 1767.

Collège Sainte-Marie (St. Mary's College), started in 1848 by the Jesuits, was intended for both French-speaking and English-speaking Roman Catholic boys.[4] These were examples of the classical college, which embraced both secondary school and university studies. Until late in the century, secondary school education provided for girls by the convent schools was not intended as a preparation for university. However, the largest of these, Villa-Maria Convent, conducted by the Congrégation de Notre Dame, proved its modernity by advertising (in 1899) that the girls had "tous les engins de gymnastique et sport sauf, jusqu'-ici, la bicyclette."

For Protestant boys there was the High School of Montreal, opened in 1843 to give a better preparation for university than that provided by the old Royal Grammar School (1818). Indeed, its founders, who were dissatisfied with McGill, hoped it would become the nucleus of another university.[5] But ten years later, the High School passed under McGill control and annually sent up its quota of young men for university entrance. In 1870, it was given a third direction: the High School was transferred to the Montreal Board of Protestant School Commissioners, the body administering the Protestant public schools of the city. The Commissioners, who had hitherto concerned themselves only with primary schools, were anxious to have a secondary school. It must be pointed out, however, that "public" did not mean "free."

This first public secondary school was followed in 1876 by a second one, also under the Protestant School Commissioners—the High School for Girls. They could then assure educational opportunity for the two sexes.[6]

Public education was twenty years established at the time of Confederation. The Education Act of 1846 had provided for two bodies of school commissioners, Roman Catholic and Protestant, nominated by the city council and the provincial government.[7] Confederation made no change in this arrangement. The problems confronting the two groups of commissioners were fundamentally the same: inadequate revenues and increasing numbers of children to care for. The elementary public schools that the commissioners operated were usually called "common schools."

The Roman Catholics were able to take advantage of the services of religious orders to staff their public schools. In 1837, the first Brothers of the Christian Schools arrived in Montreal and undertook the direction of Ecole Saint-Laurent, the largest school under the Roman Catholic Commissioners.[8] Furthermore, for nearly twenty years, 1867-86, the Commission had as chairman the Reverend Victor Rousselot, the *curé* of Notre Dame. He was a determined innovator; for example, he introduced *les jardins d'enfants,* the pioneer kindergartens in Montreal.

By the end of the nineteenth century, when the population had passed a quarter of a million, about 47,000 of whom were between the ages of five and fourteen, the number of children in the public schools had shot up enormously: in 1866, the Roman Catholics had had about a thousand and the Protestants seven hundred [9]; in 1896, the totals were 17,000 and 8,600 respectively. Impressive as these figures may seem, they included little more than half of the children of school age. A large proportion of children did not go to school at all. There was no compelling law, and with employers vigorously bidding for child labour, and with adult wages as low as they were, it must have required unusual determination to keep children at school. Children found regular jobs in textile mills (see Chapter 10), where whole families might be represented on the work force. Some of the mills engaged in recruiting campaigns in parts of the countryside where the tradition of school attendance was weak. There was, however, a brighter side: a great number of children not accounted for in the above figures went to private schools. At one point, indeed, the Protestant commission estimated that there were more children in private schools than in its own.

Some of the private schools were conducted by nondenominational organizations such as the British and Canadian School Association, founded by William Lunn, a Montrealer deeply interested in education. Others were church schools, for example, the Church of St. John the Evangelist School, the forerunner of

Lower Canada College. This school began in the little mortuary chapel in the old Protestant burying ground on Dufferin Square. A contemporary wrote: "The most striking sight in the midst of this scene of decay and desolation was a little school house, filled with merry children, who in play hours ran about among the tombs. . . . The school was a mean building . . . erected years before as a chapel or funeral house." [10] Of the non-Roman Catholic private schools in existence at Confederation, only this school survived into the next century. Though numerous, and doing the necessary work they did, the private schools had little continuity. Today, only two of the end-of-the-century schools survive—Trafalgar School for Girls, opened in 1879, and Lower Canada College.

ADULT
EDUCATION

Nor was Montreal without means of reaching those whose schooling was far behind, yet who wished to continue their education. Before the middle of the century it possessed two adult education agencies, both maintained by private funds. The older was the Mechanics' Institute, which under a slight variation in title went back to 1828.[11] A second date is of significance, 1854, when the corner stone of its building was laid. It occupied an eligible site on St. James and St. Peter streets. There were housed library, lecture hall, and classrooms. Originally, basic subjects were taught, French, English, and arithmetic; later, more technical ones, such as draughting and mechanical drawing. At a still later time, the Mechanics' Institute sponsored lectures on a variety of cultural topics. The Institute had an excellent library, probably the most widely patronized of its services.

Some sixteen years younger than the Mechanics' Institute was the Institut canadien, founded in 1844. The Institut canadien built up a fine library (it appears to have possessed the best periodical collection in

Montreal), encouraged discussion among its members, and conducted lecture programs. (Its law courses have already been mentioned.) On the eve of Confederation, the Institut and Bishop Bourget quarrelled over the refusal of the Institut to allow Church censorship of its books. When, in December 1866, the Institut canadien opened its new building on Notre Dame Street, it was therefore in a weakened condition. Nonetheless, it made a brave show; "le grand monde anglais y était représenté comme le monde canadien." Its art treasures were displayed: the classic casts given by the Emperor Napoléon III; a portrait of Galileo.[12] The picture was painted by Napoléon Bourassa and was, perhaps, a diplomatic warning that, in an earlier encounter between the Church and science, the Church had not won. Bishop Bourget, however, failed to take the hint; he denied the sacraments to its members, and it was the Institut canadien that lost. Its library was saved by being transferred to the Fraser Institute, when it was opened in 1885. The Fraser Institute was a privately endowed library, the only free one in Montreal.

In 1858, The Société Historique de Montréal was formed—the oldest historical association in Canada. Its principal founder was Montreal's first mayor, Jacques Viger. Viger was also a notable collector and displayer of historical objects, which he thought could awaken and stimulate historical interest. As early as 1859 the Société began the publication of documents. Some thirty years later (1892), it erected a monument on Place Royale to the founders of Montreal. It is pleasant to know that the Société Historique de Montréal still flourishes—now over a hundred years old.

After 1850, instruction in specialized subjects began to be supplied by other agencies. The need was particularly great for subjects required in skilled trades, where the breakdown of the apprenticeship system had left a gap. The Mechanics' Institute, as was pointed out, provided a partial bridge, with its technical and academic courses. The Council of Arts and Design (Conseil des Arts et des Métiers), set up in 1859 by the provincial government, conducted day and evening classes in both languages. Its school was much enlarged in 1872.

From its formation in 1851, the Montreal YMCA also held classes. These were greatly expanded some twenty years later, when the YMCA secured its first permanent building on Victoria Square.[13] The YMCA offered French and commercial subjects, a combination evidently intended for the young business man.

The Art Association of Montreal, formed in 1860, had teaching as one of its objectives, and instruction in some form was begun very early.[14] The opening of the Association's first art gallery in May 1879, "stand[ing] prettily out from the foliage in Phillips' Square," enabled a complete program to be put in train. By 1881, advanced classes were being conducted. The directors, drawn from the newly formed Royal Canadian Academy (1879), included Robert Harris, the author of "The Fathers of Confederation," and Douglas Brymner. In his report for 1885, Harris entered the pointed note: "The school can claim an influence extending beyond its actual walls. . . . It has modified the system [of teaching] pursued in other places. . . . That some of the students already have charge of classes of their own is evidence that the work done . . . is of a practical character."

In every one of these instances, important claims were staked out: the Montreal Technical School, opened in 1911, was derived from the classes conducted by the Conseil des Arts et des Métiers; Sir George Williams University developed from the YMCA's early evening school; the art school conducted by the Montreal Museum of Fine Arts owes its origin to the instruction begun over eighty years ago by the Art Association.

THE
NEWSPAPER
PRESS

The thirty year period after Confederation was the great age of Montreal journalism. The city supported more newspapers than it does now—sixteen in 1871—

and the newspapers were of very high calibre. Two newspaper men, Honoré Beaugrand and Alphonse Desjardins, were, respectively, the eighteenth (1885-86) and twenty-third (1893) mayors of Montreal. This bespeaks public respect for the calling.

Two newspapers were definite educational forces. The earlier was the *Daily Witness,* founded more than twenty years before Confederation, and probably at the peak of its influence then and for another eighteen years (1867-85). The owner and editor of the *Witness* was John Dougall, a Scot with a mission. He diffused the virtues of *The Cotter's Saturday Night* and preached in season and out of season the self-help doctrines of Samuel Smiles. Against these genuine services have to be set the *Witness*'s attacks on the Roman Catholic Church. The attacks largely nullified the good that the newspaper sought to do. It was only after John Dougall's death, in 1885, that the *Witness*'s prejudices abated. John Redpath Dougall, the son and successor, was an editor of very different views.

The second, and more successful, educational force was *La Presse.* Founded in 1884, by 1896 it had the largest circulation of any newspaper, not merely in Montreal but in Canada. A great deal of the success of *La Presse* may be laid to the editor-in-chief, Jules Helbronner. He was an old-country Frenchman keenly interested in economic and social problems. Helbronner turned *La Presse* into a forum for the discussion of urgent contemporary problems. *La Presse,* which employed a varied layout and pictures, was engagingly modern in format. Before the day of the half-tone illustration, newspaper pictures were usually the reproductions of pen-and-ink drawings. *La Presse* employed Henri Julien, the most brilliant black-and-white artist in Canada at that time. Nevertheless, it was as a medium of news and discussion that *La Presse* excelled and exerted its greatest influence.

The remaining newspapers had little positive significance in education. Some were violently partisan, or expressed the point of view of an individual. Examples were the *Montreal Herald* and *The Gazette* (known earlier as *The Montreal Gazette*), the two oldest papers published in Montreal—Liberal and Conservative respectively. *The Gazette* might be considered a family paper, since it was the property of the White family, having been acquired from Brown Chamberlain in 1870 by two brothers, Thomas and Richard White.[15] However, neither family interests nor idiosyncrasies were allowed to intrude.

The *Montreal Daily Star* (originally the *Evening Star* and now *The Montreal Star*) illustrated a third type— one whose prime purpose was to make money. It was established in 1869 by Hugh Graham, who in 1908 became Sir Hugh, and in 1917 was made Baron Athol-stan of Huntingdon Quebec and the City of Edinburgh. His stock-in-trade was the bizarre and sensational.[16] As proprietor, Graham dominated his newspaper and its policies. He early learned that patriotism paid; so, the *Star* was in the front of every appeal, from putting up the statue to Sir John A. Macdonald on Dominion Square to supporting the Conservative government's proposal of a gift of $35,000,000 to Britain to build battleships. Graham was an ardent crusader in municipal reform, but his motives became increasingly suspect. *The Gazette* jibed that the best way to ruin any cause in Montreal was to have the *Star* support it. Nonetheless, the *Star* prospered. By the end of the nineteenth century it could boast that it had the largest circulation of any English-language daily in Montreal. Its advertising revenue must have been the largest of any newspaper, English or French, judging from the space it commanded.

By the early 1890's commercial advertising had surpassed job-printing as the main financial support of newspapers. The Harmsworths in Britain and the Pulitzers in the United States were the first to exploit the new source. Unless some of the golden stream could be channelled off, any newspaper was doomed. In 1899, *La Minerve,* perhaps the most historically valuable of Montreal newspapers, ceased publication. It had been financed largely by government printing contracts. *La Minerve* survived by only three years the downfall of its Conservative patrons at Ottawa and Quebec. The need to provide popular material (in order to increase circulation and consequently attract more advertisers) had created a closed circle in which there was little space for the cause of education.

VICTORIAN ENTERTAINMENT

Like all people of the period, Montrealers enjoyed the lecture. It was a genuine pastime, although of an austere order. Whether it was given in "cette salle immense, longue de 80 pieds" of the Institut canadien or in more modest surroundings, Montrealers crowded in to hear a select range of local and imported talent. These included such men as the Reverend Charles Kingsley, Matthew Arnold, and Goldwin Smith.

Not all public entertainment was of a serious nature. In November 1898, Amy Redpath, the future Lady Roddick, attended the opening of Her Majesty's, on Guy Street near St. Catherine. (The Royal, which for forty years had been Montreal's chief theatre, was located away downtown, on Côté Street near Craig.) Her diary entry reads: "In the evening went with the two Miss Roddicks to the opening night at 'Her Majesty's.' The theatre was packed, everyone in their best bib and tucker. We had a box & our party consisted of also Mrs Peterson & Mrs McMaster. The theatre's pretty & tasteful but simple. The play was a sort of variety show [The Ballet Girl]. I can't understand their having such a poor performance for the opening night."

Earlier that year, without realizing the threat it posed, Miss Redpath had recorded also the appearance of the medium that would prove so damaging to the popularity of the public lecture. In April 1898, she witnessed a "cinematographic" production of the well-known Oberammergau Passion Play, shown in the Windsor Hotel: "The pictures were life-like and very beautiful & most realistic, especially when the movements were slow as in the Last Supper. The accompanying lecture was good & sometimes we were treated to solemn music in the background." [17] This appears to be an early, probably the earliest, moving picture shown in Montreal, and while not a talkie in the modern sense, it did have a sound accompaniment. It was not for another eight years that any theatre for moving pictures was opened in Montreal; nine years before a building designed especially for that purpose was put up. L. E. Ouimet began first in a converted hall, on St. Catherine Street East near Amherst, in 1906. The next year, on the same site, his "Ouimetoscope" had new luxury quarters that seated a thousand people.

In the Victorian age—before the coming of moving pictures, the radio, and television—entertainment was sustained largely by private effort. Men who formed a golf club, or who rode to hounds, might with equal facility organize a musical society, such as the Philharmonic or the Mendelssohn. Literary societies abounded. Some, such as the Athenaeum, were for the serious-minded, and drew heavily on McGill University; others were of a lighter nature. One, the Shakespeare, made a point of keeping together the city and the arts. At its annual dinner, held in April on Shakespeare's birthday, public men were always invited and were expected to speak. An invitation to the mayor was a standing one. It would be interesting to know what successive chief magistrates had to say on Shakespeare, or on the relevance of Shakespeare to Montreal.

On great occasions such as these, the club met in one of the numerous restaurants along St. James or Notre Dame. But for this organization and for many others, the home was the centre for all but the most elaborate activities. Thus there was always a strong domestic, or informal, note, which encouraged general participation. Everyone had a part, whether in speaking, singing, or acting, and success depended not upon a paid performer but upon the effort of each member.

The cultural level of Montreal was certainly less low than visiting Englishmen believed. Samuel Butler had not yet discovered his complete inability to live contentedly in any organized society, as his excursions to *Erewhon* were to show. Montreal institutions, for example its art school and the universities, had attained nation-wide celebrity. They served not only the citizens of Montreal but those of distant places, as the records of McGill University and St. Mary's College show. The former, for example, had a network of junior colleges throughout the Province of Quebec—Wesleyan College at Stanstead, St. Francis at Richmond, and Morrin at Quebec—affiliated with it. The Grand Seminary, now the theological faculty of the Université de Montréal, in the hundred years between 1840 and 1940, trained over 2600 priests for the United States, as well as nearly five thousand for Canada.[18] An achievement such as this should be kept in mind, when one is tempted to dismiss Montreal in material terms only.

9 THE POST-CONFEDERATION CITY

For at least ten years after Confederation, stability characterized Montreal life. Contemporaries might dispute the claim, in the light of their experience of a political funeral, denominational rioting, and a paralyzing depression. Nevertheless, it is true that until almost the end of the 1870's the city followed a course plotted by the achievements of 1867.

THE STRUCTURE OF THE CITY

I t was universally agreed that Montreal made the best impression from a distance and when approached by the river. Coming upstream from Quebec, one passed a number of pretty villages: Bout de l'Ile; Pointe aux Trembles; Hochelaga. Coming downstream from Ottawa there was an exciting succession of rapids that reached its climax in the Lachine. Finally, as one edged inshore to avoid the St. Mary's Current, or as one passed under the Victoria Bridge, there broke on the vision the crowded harbour of Montreal, and the city, rising in terraces towards Mount Royal. All the landmarks were clearly to be seen: the great range of the Bonsecours Market House (1846); the eccentric outlines of the City Hall (1878); and, dominating all, the twin towers of Notre Dame. What the city was and would continue to be for many years could be best seen from the St. Lawrence. Floating grain elevators lay in the shallow basins or along the low stone and wood retaining-wall that bounded the harbour. They discharged principally into sailing vessels, which, as late as 1877, formed one third of the shipping entering Montreal. Even the passenger steamships of the Allan and Dominion lines were fully rigged. A forest of masts and spars in the port matched the forest of spires and towers in the city, Dr. Victor Morin's *Ville aux clochers dans la verdure.*[1]

The city that lay behind this river base was really very small. In 1871, the population was only 107,000, and not much more than 140,000 ten years later. Its boundaries were Atwater Avenue in the west, Iberville Street in the east, and, in the north, an irregular line that included Mount Royal and then dipped south to Pine Avenue. A rectangle with its long side to the river, Montreal of the 1870's was an expansion of the ground plan imposed on it two hundred years earlier by Dollier de Casson. Movement was east and west rather than north and south. By the middle of the 1880's, the Montreal street railway had five main east and west lines and only two north and south. (For a discussion of the subject of internal transportation, see Chapter 12.)

However small Montreal would appear to modern eyes, it was remarkably diversified. The business part was confined rigidly between the river and Craig Street: wholesalers on St. Paul Street; retailers on Notre Dame and St. James. Banking was even more restricted—all in two or three blocks along St. James Street west of Place d'Armes. There were no branch banks until the Bank of Montreal established a "west end branch," whose red stone front still looms impressively on St. Catherine Street at Mansfield. The date was 1889, and this move, along with the migration to Phillips Square of two enterprising retailers, Henry Morgan and Henry Birks and Company, marked the beginning of a new era.[2]

The residential area was much more widespread. A large part of it was along St. Catherine Street itself and the cross-streets. This region lay on a plateau above the old business district and was reached by St. Denis Street, St. Lawrence Boulevard, or Beaver Hall Hill. Churches as well as people began to move to the higher level. The number built on the St. Catherine Street plateau indicates its popularity among the fortunate. The oldest and most easterly was St-Jacques-le-Majeur (mentioned in Chapter 3), the first Montreal Roman Catholic church to be consecrated as a cathedral (1825). It was twice burned, but in 1859 a third church, marked by a singularly lofty and graceful spire, was built. (Over a hundred years later, it was to be designated as the Expo 67 church for Roman Catholics and to be connected by a tunnel with the subway.) About Beaver Hall Hill there were no fewer than five churches. Just to the east, at the crest of the slope, was St. Patrick's (1847). Close to it was the Jesuit church of the Gesù, built in 1865 beside St. Mary's College. The church and college formed a very imposing pile of buildings, the church being modelled on the Gesù in Rome.[3] On Beaver Hall Hill itself were a Unitarian church, built in 1844 (the ancestor of the Church of the Messiah), Zion Congregational (1846), and St. Andrew's Presbyterian Church (1851). A little to the west, on Dorchester Street, in August 1870, Bishop Bourget blessed the cornerstone of the new Roman Catholic cathedral, St. James. The construction of this vast building, the largest in Montreal, occupied more than twenty years. It was modelled on St. Peter's in Rome; so, like the Gesù, it was a landmark both in artistic taste and in ecclesiastical temper. Then, or at a slightly later time, other churches grew up in this favoured area, St. George's (Anglican) on Dominion Square, the Dominion Square Methodist, and, more to the west, the American Presbyterian and the Crescent Street Presbyterian. Only five of these churches, St-Jacques-le-Majeur, St. Patrick's, the Gesù, St. James Cathedral, and St. George's, remain in the very different surroundings of the present day. (Only the outer walls of St-Jacques date back to 1859; fire necessitated the rebuilding of the interior in the 1930's.)

Other residential sections are less easy to locate. Place Viger (including nearby St. Denis Street) was highly regarded; so also St. Louis Square, off St. Denis north of St. Catherine. They, like St. Antoine Street, had a genuine character, a spaciousness of site and a dignity of building. On the lower easy levels west and east of the traditional limits of Montreal, McGill and Berri streets, there was a great deal of speculative building, which rapidly degenerated into slum. West and south, cut off by the Lachine canal, Pointe St. Charles, with its low tenement houses and narrow streets, was the workingman's quarter.

A strong element of uniformity was visible in house design throughout these widely separated regions of Montreal. The terrace was, by the late 1860's, accepted. From the builder's point of view, it had the advantage of making the best use of the site; from the occupant's, warmth, since only the front and rear walls were exposed. A height of three, or at most four, storeys was preferred. The basement contained the kitchen, various storerooms, and, frequently, the bathroom. On the ground floor were dining and living rooms. The second floor had bedrooms and, sometimes, an upstairs living room. A larger house might repeat this arrangement on a third floor. Finally, the top floor provided storage space, drying rooms for laundry in winter, and rooms for the servants. The layout was inconvenient in the extreme. Such houses were gloomy, since light entered only at the front and the back, and probably cold, since central-heating by furnace was not yet common. (The passage of the domestic year was marked by the putting up and taking down of stoves and their pipes.) There were variations of the plan for people in modest circumstances; so the terraced house, fortress-like in appearance, was widespread. It was this vision of endless houses that made such a lasting impression on the child Wilfrid Laurier, when he was taken through Montreal in 1849.

On the plateau were found the chief parks of the city. In the early 1870's, Montreal secured the Protestant and Roman Catholic burying grounds and formed them into Dufferin and Dominion squares. (New cemeteries had been acquired: Mount Royal for Protestants, in 1852; Côte des Neiges for Roman Catholics, in 1855.) In 1873, the city made a really splendid gain of a park area on Mount Royal. The eastern part of the city was less well provided for, although in 1873 the federal government permitted the formation of a park on St. Helen's Island. Fifteen years later (1888), what is now known as Parc LaFontaine (formerly a military reserve) was made over by the same authority; thus the amenities of west and east were balanced. The establishment of the parks was a blessing to Montreal and certainly a most creditable action on the part of the civic administration. (The example of Central Park,

New York, was very much in mind.) The initiative was taken by a small group of French-Canadian public men all more or less connected with *La Minerve*.

THE TEMPER
OF THE TIMES
COMMERCIAL,
MILITARY,
AND SPORTING

A commercial outlook dominated Montreal. The ideal citizen was the merchant, and immense deference was paid to his views. The merchants were effectively organized in the Montreal Board of Trade, which was incorporated under that title in 1841, although it had been in existence as the Committee of Trade for nearly twenty years (1822).[4] The Board was the arm of the French-Canadian and Anglo-Canadian mercantile oligarchy and was primarily interested in overseas trade. It had two allies, the Corn Exchange (1862), and the Chambre de Commerce du District de Montréal (1886).[5] The Corn Exchange reflected the growing interest of Montrealers in speculation in cereals. The Chambre de Commerce spoke for the French-Canadian merchant and also for the French-Canadian manufacturer. At that time, the Chambre attracted the support of men interested in Quebec or Canadian trade, in contrast to overseas trade. The three were "the public bodies," as they liked to call themselves. Widely representative and fully supported, they wielded a powerful influence that made itself felt in the city council, the Quebec legislature, and the Canadian parliament. Dr. (later Sir William) Hingston, the mayor, stated an accepted fact when he declared, in 1877, that the city council would ever seek to promote the commercial interests as interpreted by "the public bodies."

The remark was provoked by the strike of the Grand Trunk locomotive engineers, December 1876.[6] Relations between employees and management had been bad. Men were fined or laid off for trivial offences.

There was constant threat of a cut in wages. Although the engineers were well paid, the highest class receiving $2.50 a day, their calling was a trying and dangerous one. On December 7, the blow fell. Wage cuts were posted and many received discharge notices. The men enjoyed considerable sympathy until they struck, two weeks later. When, however, trains ceased moving, there was an outcry from the commercial classes, whose profits were interfered with. The Montreal city council ranged itself on the side of the outraged business men. (At the end of about a week the Railway agreed to take the strikers back at their former wage, but made no other concessions.)

Another aspect of the contemporary outlook was an interest in militia service. "Volunteering" was the phrase employed, and it perfectly conveyed the idea, the uncovenanted offer of service and time to the defence of Canada. The alarms of the Civil War and of the Fenian Raids that followed had introduced a sense of urgency, which the withdrawal of the last British regulars from Montreal about 1870 had done nothing to allay. Young men of what might be described as the professional and mercantile classes were those that felt most strongly the obligation to serve. It is worth noting that two men of such generally divergent views as Wilfrid Laurier and Honoré Mercier both obtained commissions and did duty as militia officers.

Among both French and English Roman Catholic Montrealers, the martial spirit was heightened by the exploits of the young men who had defended the Holy See against the Italians. The papal zouave in his grey uniform, with its scarlet flashes and jaunty képi, was a familiar and honoured figure in Montreal streets. The returns of the two major zouave contingents in the spring and autumn of 1870 were occasions for widespread popular manifestation. The prompt offer of zouave service against the impending Fenian invasion, in April 1870, was a recommendation to which even English Protestant Montreal could not be indifferent. By that date, there were twelve volunteer military units in Montreal, one of which, the Victoria Rifles, carried its same designation until its disbandment in 1965. At various crises, the volunteers appeared in impressive numbers. In 1875, a fraction of the Montreal force provided over a thousand men for the preservation of domestic peace. Ten years later, the *65ᵉ bataillon,* known today as the Fusiliers de Mont-Royal, along with another unit no longer in existence, saw service on distant Saskatchewan battlefields.

Nevertheless, it was in the day-to-day life of the city that the volunteer made his greatest contribution. His brief free time during the week (the age was one of the six-day week and the ten-hour day) was given to nightly drills; his short summer holiday, to annual camps on St. Helen's Island or at Laprairie. He did distasteful police duty to prop up "the civil power" at times of emergency. In the smallpox epidemic of 1885, he played nurse. Families developed hereditary attachment to various units, sons following fathers in the ranks or in the commissioned grades. The volunteer soldier was an established figure on the civic landscape, just as volunteering was a recognized expression of civic virtue.

From soldiering to sports, the transition was easy; all too easy in the view of the serious-minded. The militia regiments had active sports interests, which, in turn, strengthened the urge towards organization of amateur athletics. Equally accurate, would be this statement in reverse, since some of the athletic clubs provided the nuclei of Montreal regiments. The Lacrosse Club, for example, contributed no fewer than five companies to the Victoria Rifles, and this was by no means unusual. The emphasis was on amateurism and on group participation. Clubs catered to every interest: lacrosse; cricket; snowshoeing. The oldest appears to have been the Lacrosse Club, formed in 1856. In 1882, an important amalgamation took place with the formation of the Montreal Amateur Athletic Association, initially a federation of five clubs.

The most popular summer and autumn sports were cricket, lacrosse, and football. Tennis had not yet attained the status of a competitive sport or one that lent itself to organization. It, along with croquet and archery, was thought of as a garden game, played for entertainment. In 1874, there was the sudden rise of a new sport—bicycling. It was duly organized into a club, the Montreal Bicycle Club, in 1878. It sponsored "long rides of two or three days' duration . . . even to Toronto 330 miles distant." These must have been gruelling, since the bicycles employed were "the pennyfarthings" (more realistically known as "bone-shakers"), which were springless and had a big wheel in front and a small wheel behind. When, a little later, "the safety" appeared—the ancestor of the modern bicycle—it was derided by the tough veterans, as fit only for women.

In the winter, many turned to snowshoeing. There were tramps over Mount Royal for the sedate and obstacle races for the daring. Tobogganing was an auxiliary of snowshoeing; literally so, when (in 1883) the Tuque Bleue snowshoe club organized a Tuque Bleue toboggan club. Curling, however, was the most popular of winter sports, as also, one of the oldest. It was effectively organized, such clubs as the Royal Montreal and the Thistle being well established even in the 1870's.

Winter sports lent themselves to exploitation by hotels and shopkeepers and by the railways. At various times during the 1870's and 1880's, winter carnivals were held. They embraced all the popular sporting events and had as their symbol an ice palace on Dominion Square. The storming of this edifice, by assorted snowshoers, tobogganers, and other merry-makers, formed the climax of the carnival. The carni-vals became increasingly elaborate and costly and were abandoned in 1889.

Montreal was celebrated for two other sports, hunt-ing and golf. The Montreal Hunt, earlier known as the Montreal Fox Hounds, was, in fact, the oldest of the city's sporting organizations, dating back to 1826.[7] In the decade or so after Confederation, it enjoyed great vigour and popularity. Rather to the dismay of the serious hunting men, it became a centre for social life. Golf was much more recent, but by 1873 it had attained sufficient support to warrant the setting up of a club— the Royal Montreal Golf Club, to employ the modern title. Both the Hunt and the golf club are of historical significance. They anticipated later developments in sports, in that they provided a spectacle for onlookers and an opportunity for social gathering. Both admitted women and thus foreshadowed a further development, the participation of women in vigorous outdoor sports. Finally, since both hunting and golf, in their Canadian expression, originated in Montreal, they gave the city a primacy. At least one other hunting organization, the London Hunt and Country Club, was founded on the model of the Montreal Hunt. This suggests that "metropolis," as applied to Montreal, has more than the usual economic or political connotation.

Time has worked strange reverses in sports-fashions. Cricket, looked upon as one of the most popular of Montreal summer sports, scarcely merits that description today. Baseball, which currently probably stands highest, was introduced almost surreptitiously at the end of the 1860's. Tradition has it that baseball came in with the return of the young French Canadians who had learned to like the game during the Civil War. In 1892, basketball was first played in Montreal. It had been designed a year before by James Naismith, a Montreal YMCA worker, who wished to produce an indoor game that called for speed and accuracy. From that modest beginning, basketball was to become, literally, world-wide in its popularity.

A
PERIOD OF
CIVIC STRIFE

Events of the later 1870's shattered the appearance of stability and domestic order. By 1875, Montreal had experienced at least two years of business depression and its grim accompaniments, unemployment and destitution. Except for the brief recession of 1857-58, this appears to have been Montreal's only experience with hard times for twenty years. Temporary fallings-off of business there had been, but none as sustained as that which set in with the autumn of 1873. It affected Montreal and its hinterland, the Ottawa valley, where the lumber trade was paralysed and where farming was in jeopardy from successive droughts. By

1875, the very large number of Montrealers who were casual labourers on the docks, or carters in the town, were in a desperate plight. The autumn of 1875 witnessed "the bread riots." The destitute surrounded the city hall, crying, "We are hungry. We want food." The passage of a baker's cart and a brewer's dray dissolved the mob, which "had a good drink and cleaned out the cart." The chief constable, thereupon, fell on the poor people and drove them along Notre Dame Street with his cane. Such was the backcloth for the sharp and serious clashes of the late 1870's—clashes in which religious, racial, and economic tensions were all intermingled.

In the late autumn of 1875, Joseph Guibord was finally buried in Côte des Neiges Cemetery, fully six years after his death. The protracted obsequies were occasioned by the kind of feud that could occur only in a divided community such as Montreal was. The root was the quarrel between the Roman Catholic bishop, Mgr Ignace Bourget, and the Institut canadien, whose library contained prohibited books. Guibord had refused to give up his membership, as Roman Catholics were required to do, and, in consequence, was denied the sacraments. Following his death in 1869, he had been refused ecclesiastical burial in his family plot in Côte des Neiges. The body was placed temporarily in a vault in the Mount Royal Cemetery, while his friends of the Institut took up the quarrel. Since they were lawyers, they made the best of it, carrying their case, finally, to the Judicial Committee of the Imperial Privy Council. The decision of this tribunal opened the Cemetery. In spite of the court order, the first attempt to bury Guibord, in September of 1875, was blocked by what was, with some restraint, described as "a turbulent mob." The gates of the Cemetery were closed in defiance of the law, and the pathetic burial party trailed back to Mount Royal. Two months later (November), elaborate steps were taken to uphold the majesty of the law. A militia force, numbering about a thousand, mustered before the Craig Street Armoury and moved by way of St. Lawrence Boulevard and what today is Mount Royal Avenue. It must have been a Hogarthian scene, to judge from contemporary representations: the troops—cavalry, artillery, and infantry—marching along the sodden roads; spectators lining the route or crowding the windows of nearby houses. The troops were halted about a mile from Mount Royal Cemetery. Under the direction of the mayor, Dr. Hingston, Guibord's body was removed from the vault. A police detachment, forty of them armed, had been provided to escort the hearse. The mayor preceded the *cortège* to Côte des Neiges where burial took place. Occasion to bring the militia into the scene did not arise, and when possible need was past, the troops continued their march, going by the Cemetery, and down Côte des Neiges Road. The show of force was probably quite unnecessary, for Bishop Bourget had prepared an effective riposte. He caused Guibord's grave to be deconsecrated.

The later disturbances of the period had a character of their own. Early July was ever a time of effervescence in Montreal, with the Irish community lapsing into its traditional divisions. The parade of Protestants on July 12, the Orange Walk, stirred varied (and often violent) passions. In 1877, as an aftermath of the Walk, a young Orangeman was killed in broad daylight on Victoria Square. The victim, John Hackett, was himself armed, and an eye-witness testified: "Everyone seemed to have a revolver." It was, therefore, to the highest degree provocative to propose a parade on July 12, 1878. In spite of the appeal of the Anglican bishop and the other Protestant clergy, the Orangemen persisted with their plan and let it be understood that they would have the support of lodges outside Montreal. Confronted with a challenge of this kind, the city council banned the Walk. The Orangemen, or a group of them, thereupon defied the order. In consequence, the County Master and the parade marshal were arrested, and the rank-and-file sent home to safety in hansom cabs. Montreal's "Orange riot," in contrast to New York's of a decade before, ended very much in an anticlimax. However, this happy ending should not conceal the fact that over two thousand troops had stood to arms, and five hundred special constables had been sworn in.

The summer of 1878 safely past, tensions apparently

relaxed. By winter Montreal had so completely recovered its accustomed urbanity that the youthful Governor General, the Marquis of Lorne, and his even more youthful wife, Princess Louise, were able to indulge in a thrilling midnight adventure. "Louise dressed somewhat as a *habitant* with dress tucked up and veil drawn closely down: the Marquis completely disguised in very common clothes with pants turned up and slouched hat . . . walked through the streets." The change in temper may have resulted from the hope that political change often brings. In the autumn of 1878 there had been fought the most significant federal election between Confederation and 1896. Montreal joined in the triumph of the Conservatives and their National Policy. There were splendid illuminations in the office of *La Minerve* and a grand torchlight procession the length of St. James Street. The latter was in honour of Thomas White, the owner of *The Gazette.* Although he had been elected for Cardwell, an Ontario constituency, he was popularly regarded as the parliamentary spokesman for Montreal's interests. The march of progress, it was felt, had been resumed.

10 "THE CITY BELOW THE HILL"

In the 1880's and 1890's, it was said, Montreal was a very pleasant place to live in. Doubtless it was, if you could choose in what part of it you would live. By 1892, Confederation was a quarter of a century in the past. A new generation had grown up. This is an appropriate point at which to consider Montreal in the experience of the mass of its people.

WORK, WAGES, AND LIVING

Work was hard and hours were long. These terms apply right across the wide range of industrial and commercial activity. Although some employers prided themselves on introducing labour-saving devices, these did not materially cut down on work, nor did they shorten hours. By the workers themselves, machinery was often looked upon with suspicion, since it frequently led to speed-up or to the employment of unskilled or semi-skilled labour. It was also dangerous: "Gearing, fly-wheels, pulleys, belts, and steam engines are . . . entirely unprotected." Such was the burden of evidence of the employees who appeared in Montreal before two federal commissions; one in 1882, to inquire into the working of mills and factories, the other in 1888, on the relations of capital and labour.

Large numbers of women and children were employed. Older male workers in tobacco or textiles lamented the invasion of these industries that at one time were man's preserve. Children might begin work as early as eight or ten years of age. A large family, an employer complacently remarked, was an asset.[1] The first provincial legislation for the protection of workers (passed in 1885) specified that dangerous machinery must be guarded, separate privies for men and women provided, and the written consent of the parent or guardian secured for the employment of boys under eleven and of girls under fourteen. (With consent, there was no minimum age.) The hours per day, in the case of children only, were limited to ten. The onerous provisions of this measure were much deplored by the employers who appeared before the Royal Commission.

The ten-hour day (established first in 1840 by the United States Government for its own employees) was for most workers everywhere still an ideal to be achieved rather than a reality to be enjoyed. Clerks in retail stores were expected to arrive early to lay out stock and to stay late to make up their accounts. They had no legal right to redress, if they were required to work beyond the six-day week. The traditional "late Saturday night" frequently extended well into Sunday morning before stock was taken and the last penny accounted for. In the metal industry, the heating of a furnace determined the length of the work time.[2] A man who loaded coal testified before the Royal Commission of 1888 as follows:

Q.—Have you known any men who have done more than twenty-four hours consecutively?   A.— . . . And as for me, I have worked since yesterday morning until six o'clock this evening.

Q.—That makes 36 hours? A.—Yes; I had my dinner hours, and that made 30 hours of work.

Q.—You got no extra pay for that? A.—No extra pay, in the course of the winter.

. . . .

A.—. . . The foreman does not remain with us during the night, because we are driven by work, and the work must be done, or we are reported the next morning.

For all jobs entailing manual labour, the numbers available were large. Competition was desperate, whether among the skilled or the unskilled. Conversely, clerical staffs were small, and limited in sex. To the end of the 1890's, the office-worker was a man. Typewritten records, which became common in the nineties, were made by men. In the experience of Montreal, the upward path of women was through new services such as the telephone exchange. It was the switchboard, not the keyboard, that emancipated the woman worker.

Such a field might seem fully ripe for action by a vigorous working class. There was virtually none. Montreal labour did not produce leadership from its own ranks. From outside the ranks, only three men (all lawyers) gave anything more than passing interest: Médéric Lanctôt, in the early 1870's; Adolphe Chapleau, in the late 1870's; and Raymond Préfontaine, in the 1890's. Lanctôt has been aptly characterized as "a national socialist before national socialism."[3] In eastern Montreal, he organized co-operatives, for example, stores and loan societies. Chapleau's interest was less localized. He affected to speak for all organized labour. Both men allowed themselves to be turned away by political ambitions—Lanctôt to the Liberals, Chapleau to the Conservatives. It is possible that at a later date Chapleau found it politically advantageous to revive his interest in labour: there is evidence that he tried to ingratiate himself with the Knights of Labour. Préfontaine, like the other two, had ambitions besides the leadership of the working class: the city council; the mayoralty; the House of Commons; and the federal cabinet. It is impossible to escape the conclusion that for all three men the championing of labour was in some degree a means to other ends.

No purely Montreal labour group, owing allegiance only to the local organization, seems to have survived to the end of the century. (Associations such as the Union St-Joseph, formed among stone-cutters, were mutual benefit societies.) Only when attached to some international body could organized labour hold its own. There were further weaknesses in the local groups. The craft unions appealed only to skilled men. Moreover, they were often divided on racial lines; for example, among printers and carpenters there were locals for both French- and English-speaking members. The strongest unions were those among cigar workers, and these were strong, only because of the industry's complete dependence upon the skilled hand-worker.

For a time, it appeared that the Knights of Labour would surmount all disabilities: they were an international body; they admitted skilled and unskilled; and they united the two language groups.[4] The Knights entered Montreal in the 1870's, probably first among railwaymen. At the beginning of the 1880's there were three assemblies, or locals. By 1885, there were twenty-two; by 1887, thirty-eight. This was the high point, and this was the period when Chapleau displayed his greatest concern for the Knights. They rapidly declined in membership. In 1891 there were only four assemblies in Montreal.

Initiative returned to the craft unions. They were much better equipped to exercise it, now that they had submitted to federation in the Trades and Labour Congress. Like its counterpart, the American Federation of Labour, the TLC was conservative, asking merely for its share of the cake. By the end of the 1890's, it had achieved a recognized position. Labour Day (instituted in 1882) was celebrated for the first time in Montreal in 1887 and was marked by a parade for the first time the next year. Montreal labour was the reverse of class-conscious, and the spirit of its organization as far removed from revolutionáry European syndicalism as the first of September is from May Day.

Wages varied a good deal, although they had one thing in common: they were low. The best wages went to railway workers, especially to those in the running trades. This was the happy result of over thirty years of patient pressure by the brotherhoods, the railway unions, organized on craft lines.[5] It might be noted, parenthetically, that no Montreal railwaymen appear to have been attracted towards Eugene Debs' general railway union. Possibly this saved Montreal unionism from a disaster similar to that experienced by the Chicago unions in 1896, following the strike. Other labour on railway pay rolls seems to have done well. Unskilled labour employed by the Canadian Pacific ordinarily received twenty-five cents a day more than the going rate for such labour. At the other extreme were the wages paid to textile and tobacco workers. Their wages were depressed by the extensive employment of women and children, and by the introduction of machinery. It was asserted before the Royal Commission that wages in these occupations had not advanced from the level of thirty years before, in spite of the enormously greater productivity. The plight of the workers was made even worse by the common practice of reducing wages during the winter, when competition was keenest.

The working man's (or the working woman's) lot was not a happy one. In fact, it was less happy than it had been or was to be. Industry in the 1890's was impersonal, partly because of the numbers employed, but much more because of the attitude of the employing class. Labour was looked upon simply as a commodity to be bought in the cheapest markets. "It is a matter of supply and demand," said the future Sir William Macdonald (at that time spelled McDonald), in his appearance before the Royal Commission. At an earlier time, the employer had felt a moral responsibility toward his work force; at a later time, organized labour was able to command respect. In the period under examination, only one Montreal firm appears to have made a genuine effort to work harmoniously with labour. Ames-Holden, the shoe manufacturer, recognized the union as a negotiating agent and used the union label on its products.

It is not surprising that a good many Montrealers lived near subsistence level. Poverty was an accepted fact of life, to be alleviated by private effort. The national societies and the churches bore the brunt of assistance. The Roman Catholic Church, through its religious orders (with their strong instinct for social service), reached a wide circle of poor; so too did the Salvation Army, whose operations in "darkest Montreal" began in 1884. Three years later, 1887, General Booth himself opened the first Montreal headquarters. Strange anomalies sometimes appeared. An illustration is provided by the distribution of the firewood brought by *curé* Labelle and his parishioners. Half of it was given to French Roman Catholics, one-quarter to Irish Roman Catholics, and the remaining quarter was divided among all the charitable organizations. The Protestant poor, as such, were left out in the cold.

The dividing lines of Montreal were those imposed by economic circumstance and social position. The picture of a "French" Montreal and an "English" Montreal is less than realistic. There were two Montreals, the city on the hill and "the city below the hill." The latter phrase was coined by Herbert Brown Ames, of the Ames-Holden shoe company mentioned above. At this point he makes his appearance as a pioneer sociologist and civic reformer.[6] He was born to an assured position, the son of Evans F. Ames, a New Englander who established a shoe factory in Montreal. From this advantageous base, Herbert Ames was to make his way into Montreal municipal politics and into the federal parliament, in each setting always taking the progressive line. In 1897, Ames published the study *The City below the Hill.* The area examined lay south of the Canadian Pacific railway line and between Bleury Street and the western city limits. Here Ames and his associates conducted their detailed studies of wages, housing, and family structure. Many of the findings could be applied to other sections of the city, notably to St. Mary's and St. Jean Baptiste wards, but Ames was at once too honest and too pedestrian to attempt broad generalizations. His city below the hill was the home of the manual workers. Judged by contemporary standards, they were by no means ill-paid, but they were, nonetheless, unable to secure many of the amenities and even some of the decencies of life. Low wages and the lack of cheap, speedy transportation constrained the workers to live in the midst of "tall chimnies . . . and such evidences of industry [that] the air hangs heavy with their smoke." There was much over-crowding, houses or tenements being built behind each other. "Drainage" (Ames's term for sewage disposal) was primitive in the extreme. Although Montreal had a fine water system, the outdoor privy was common in this district, sharing with the communal water tap the narrow space between ranges of tenements. That homely object, the outdoor privy, was regarded by Ames and his fellow reformers as the symbol of civic decadence, and their battle cry became "The privy pit must go."

Health conditions throughout the city were deplorable.[7] It was customary to attribute much of this to the weather. No attempt was made to clear away the winter snow, with the consequence that debris and offal that had collected in it lay in the streets and lanes well into summer. In the face of conditions such as these, and a wide-spread fatalism, the city Department of Health could do little. It was ill-paid and undermanned. The passage of the year was marked by outbreaks of typhoid fever in spring and smallpox in the autumn. In 1879, when an unusually virulent smallpox epidemic threatened, the Board of Trade embarked on a campaign of public education. It was conducted with due regard to local peculiarities. "The best way of influencing the Masses," the committee of the Board advised, "would be for the Mayor to call a meeting of the Roman Catholic clergy, in your office at an hour when members of the press could be most *conveniently prevented* from attending." Six years later, smallpox again reached epidemic proportions. The outbreak of 1885 raged throughout the summer and into the autumn. The first cases, brought into the city by railway travellers, were reported in February. They were promptly isolated, and this measure appeared to be effective. Unfortunately, some of the early victims were released prematurely and so carried the disease into Montreal. By June, the attack seemed to be mastered, and it was believed that the danger had passed. In July, the smallpox suddenly reasserted itself in a most virulent form. By late autumn, it had claimed well over 2,500 victims. The densely populated sections of the city suffered most heavily. This was especially true of the northeastern part, where, as has been stated, conditions resembling those in Ames's "city below the hill" prevailed. In the accompanying panic, there was resistance to isolation and vaccination measures. The mayor, Honoré Beaugrand, showed great resolution in the crisis (without regard for his later municipal career)—the Montreal troops returning from the Saskatchewan Rebellion found themselves drafted as sanitary police.

THE FRENCH
AND
ENGLISH WORLDS

Across the years, the population of Montreal
rose steadily. From slightly over 155,000 in 1881, it
reached well over 267,000 in 1901. Although the later
figure included early annexations—Hochelaga and St.
Gabriel—the increase was striking. Montreal was
passing into the category of the large city. It far out-
distanced any Canadian rival and maintained a high
place among large North American cities. The metropolis was clearly in the making.

The most significant feature of the growing Montreal
population was its increasingly French-Canadian nature.
By the beginning of the 1870's, French Canadians had
re-established their numerical superiority—some 57,000
French Canadians to 48,000 English. Ten years later,
the margin had greatly widened, and by 1901 French
Canadians formed nearly sixty-one per cent of the
population. Furthermore, they predominated in every
section of the city except two, the southwest and the
west. Even there, they formed about one half the total.

An interesting and important feature of French-
Canadian Montreal was the degree to which it was
recruited from the outside. All seven of the French-
Canadian mayors between 1879 and 1902—Rivard,
Beaudry, Beaugrand, Grenier, Desjardins, Villeneuve,
and Préfontaine—were born outside Montreal.[8] So were
many other members of the city council and administration. At a slightly later date (1904), the mayor, Hormisdas Laporte, was not a native Montrealer, nor were
twenty of the twenty-five French-Canadian aldermen.
This may have have been exceptional, but it shows that
French-Canadian Montreal was constantly reinforced
from outside. The city acted as a magnet for the ambitious and the able. Montreal was enriched and the
French-Canadian community strengthened by this
strong current of immigration.

It was not so with the other major element of the
Montreal population. The English increased in number,

but not so as to maintain their proportional footing. By 1901, they formed only about thirty-five per cent. Moreover, they were not evenly spread throughout the city. Where they were concentrated in the west and south, they constituted a small majority; in the centre of Montreal, they formed a considerable minority; in the new parts of the city, as it grew east and northeast, they were merely small enclaves.

In many respects, English Montreal was a miniature version of French Montreal. It had its classes and masses, the latter proportionately much smaller. The English wage-earners, so Ames believed, were among the best paid and the worst paid in Montreal. The unskilled English worker tended to be squeezed out. In a wrangle in the city council in the late 1880's over winter work, James McShane stood up for a fair deal for the Irish Roman Catholic poor. George Washington Stephens Sr., an English-speaking non-Roman Catholic, stood up for the same group—"not for the Protestant Englishman or Scotsman, for there were but few." It was probably not an inaccurate statement, and it concealed the real tragedy of the minority. The English-speaking working man was caught between the upper and nether millstones—competition for jobs with the French Canadians and indifference to his fate on the part of his own racial group. Stephens's remark bears out the old complaint that no poor were worse off than the Protestant poor of Montreal. It is on points such as this that the similarities between French and English Montreal begin to break down. It is hard to imagine that any late nineteenth-century French-Canadian Montrealer would be indifferent to the misfortunes of other French-Canadian Montrealers. The two communities were basically unlike, the English being divided within itself on denominational and (for lack of a better term) national lines. Fissuring such as this made effective combination in any field impossible. The Irish, who were divided denominationally from the other English-speaking elements and linguistically from their French co-religionists, looked after their unfortunates with sturdy independence. During the long pastorate of the Reverend Patrick Dowd, 1863-91, St. Patrick's congregation provided itself with a high school, two elemen-

tary schools, an orphans' home, and a refuge for old
people. This was a mark for others to shoot at. Inevitably the effectiveness of English Protestant Montreal
effort was weakened by its internal division.

THE BEGINNING
OF
MULTIRACIALISM

The last twenty years of the nineteenth century witnessed new figures on the social landscape—Montrealers who were neither French nor British in origin.
They were Russians, Syrians, and Italians. This was the
first appearance of other races in large numbers.

The Russians were Jews, who had been uprooted
from their old home in western Russia by the bitter
persecutions that began in 1881. By 1900, six thousand
had reached Montreal, to be added to the already
established Jewish community of about eight hundred.
Elements of the latter group went back at least to the
Cession. Because they were English-speaking, having
come from Britain or the American Colonies, they were
indistinguishable (in the secular sense) from the general English community. In the middle years of the
nineteenth century, German Jews had settled in Montreal. They were part of the migration from central
Europe that followed the ending of the French Revolution and the Napoleonic Wars. Since many of them had
come by way of the United States, they, too, were
absorbed by English Montreal. The task of caring for
the Russian newcomers was borne by the established
Jewish community, through its charitable and educational organizations. These received aid from outside,
for example, from the European Jewish philanthropist
the Baron de Hirsch, in whose honour the Montreal
Jewish centre, The Baron de Hirsch Institute, was
named. It was opened in 1891 on St. Elizabeth Street.
Eleven years later, 1902, a fine new building for the
Institute was dedicated. It formed a landmark for many
years on Bleury Street.[9]

The other groups—Syrians and Italians—were Roman Catholic, and it was the Roman Catholic Church that set up missions for them in 1892 and 1893. The spiritual needs of the Italians (some fourteen hundred by 1893) were first overseen by Canon Paul Bruchési, who in 1897 became the second archbishop of Montreal. Although the Syrians were fewer in numbers, probably totalling no more than two or three hundred, they received a priest of their own nationality. He and the Italian priest who followed Canon Bruchési were the first non-French, non-English clergymen to minister permanently in Montreal.

In the historic sense, the new arrivals had a special significance: they marked the breakdown of the simple division of Montreal on bi-racial lines. The modern multi-racial city began to form in the last years of the 1890's.

11 MUNICIPAL GOVERNMENT

PART II: LA MARÉE AMÉRICAINE

For at least twenty years after Confederation, city government trod familiar ways. The period was generally stable, apart from the slow erosion of the English-speaking part of the population. There was little occasion for spirited action. Another element in the lack of change was the character of the Montreal electorate. The political nation, that is to say, the enfranchised and interested part of the population, was very small. Property qualification limited the number of voters, and failure to pay taxes disqualified many of that already small number. As late as the middle 1880's, when new forces were beginning to shake the city—now with a population of almost 200,000—it was reported that, of the 31,400 voters, 17,931 were disqualified because of arrears in tax payments. Only about half of the qualified voters went to the polls in 1886 to decide whether Honoré Beaugrand should have a second term as mayor, despite the fact that he was the type of man who roused strong feeling. He had taken a decisive stand during the smallpox epidemic of 1885, enforcing regulations with a fine disregard for his personal popularity.[1] The city's official title till 1874, that of the Corporation of the City of Montreal, accurately stated its legal structure. The corporation was the small group of enfranchised citizens—not the mass of people who lived in the city. Even the change of title in 1874 to the City of Montreal did not confer full citizenship upon the general populace.

The mayor and council formed the head of city government. As explained in Chapter 4, the mayoralty had become an office of dignity, rather than one of power. (In the thirty years following Confederation, there were only two outstanding exceptions, Honoré Beaugrand, already referred to, and Sir John C. Abbott. (Abbott was one of the ablest lawyers of his day, Dean of Law at McGill, and a future Prime Minister of Canada.) Convention required that the mayoralty should alternate between a French Canadian and an

Anglo-Canadian. There was nothing rigid in the arrangement, and a popular or capable man might serve several terms of office. English Montreal was certainly the gainer, in view of its declining numbers. The council rapidly secured the grip in administration. This was especially so after 1874, when the council was organized in various executive committees, which had oversight of roads, finance, police, public health, and so on. The committee chairmen became the decisive municipal figures. They had the real power. The committee system was often likened to the cabinet system in the federal or provincial governments. There was one enormous difference. There was no prime minister and, therefore, no effective co-ordination and control.

City government has its administrative as well as its legislative side. Slowly Montreal built up an administrative cadre. Wages were low; interference from the council was frequent. In a general way, those services that were essential to the protection of property fared best. The fire department had highest priority. Four years before Confederation, Montreal had formally set up a fire department of its own. Before that time, it had depended on volunteer fire companies, whose rivalry and inefficiency probably contributed to the long toll of disastrous fires. (At the time of the burning of the Parliament House in 1849, one cut another's fire hose.) The first departmental chief was Alexander Bertram, who found time to compose an exciting memoir, *Fighting the Flames*.[2] Bertram appears to have had real talent for coaxing money to buy equipment. Nevertheless, he had a long struggle to secure steam fire-engines, in spite of the fact that hand-powered pumps were no longer able to reach the tops of many buildings—five or six storeys high by the 1870's.

The police did less well than the fire department. As crime was of a simple homicidal sort and rarely endangered property, it was felt that the police could be safely neglected. The force was undermanned and underpaid. (As late as 1885, a constable received only nine dollars a week.) The composition of the police reflected the racial and denominational make-up of the city. At the time of the Orange riots, the police numbered two hundred men. One hundred were French Roman Catholics; fifty were Irish Roman Catholics; forty-eight were Anglo-Protestants; and two were French-Canadian Protestants. High priority was given to recruits secured from the Royal Irish Constabulary. However, as the only men Montreal was likely to get from that famous force were either deserters or men who had been dismissed, the standard was not high. In times of stress, such as the Guibord funeral or the Orange riots, the militia might be called in. This was expensive. Accordingly, reliance was usually placed on special constables, recruited from (so it was optimistically hoped) respectable and law-abiding citizens.

Other services, notably that of public health, did even less well. All departments complained of interference from the executive committees. Probably some of the interference was justified. On the other hand, much of it appears to have been petty in the extreme. Montreal was destined to wait a long time before it secured an efficient municipal civil service.

FRANCHISES AND ANNEXATIONS

Across the years, the business that the council was called upon to do increased enormously in volume and complexity. Perhaps recognizing its inability to cope with much of it, the council left large areas to private enterprise. After its venture in municipally owned water supply, the council undertook to provide no further public utilities. In the 1850's, it is true, the city considered supplying gas.[3] Gas was used for street-lighting and, increasingly, for the domestic purposes of cooking and illumination. The project of municipal gas supply was finally dropped. Transportation, communications, and power all remained private domains.

The suppliers of these services secured what was usually called a franchise. The term has a hard North American ring. The franchise carried with it numerous privileges: monopoly in the service performed; determination of charges; right of expropriation. Franchises, which were granted by the city council, were eagerly sought after. Interested franchise-seekers lobbied vigorously, and frequently went far beyond that. Councillors learned (some, doubtless, required little teaching) that every man was supposed to have his price.

Two franchises were of the utmost importance. One dealt with transportation; the other, with electric power supply. The City Passenger Railway had carried on an active lobbying campaign to secure its right to operate in 1861. There had been rivals, but it was clear that the Montreal group, which could cite the success of the Lachine Rail-Road, had the advantage. The company never allowed it to slip and, at every renewal or need for track extension, sought a further advantage. The company had the outlying sections of the city and the suburbs at its mercy. The fares levied were heavy items in the budgets of working-class families. By refusing to build, or by building only in certain directions, the street railway could dictate the pattern of growth. In the pre-motor-car age, the street railway was one of the most potent factors in the growth of Montreal, as it was in the lives of Montrealers. Members of the city council who represented the outlying wards became spokesmen for the City Passenger Railway. They had to secure transportation for their constituents at whatever terms the company would offer. The company's hand, already powerful, was greatly strengthened in the decade following 1883. The annexation of various suburbs, beginning with Hochelaga, increased the areas of the city dependent on transportation. (Since Hochelaga contained the stables and car barns of the City Passenger Railway, it was, for political purposes, a street railway preserve.) The electrification of the railway (completed in 1894) greatly increased its utility, and therefore the leverage that it could apply.[4]

The electric power franchise followed a somewhat similar course. Electricity for commercial use was introduced into Montreal by the Royal Electric Company. Immediately, there was an agitation for its use in street lighting. A three-way struggle developed between the

Royal Electric, a rival electric company, and the entrenched City Gas Company. The Royal won and secured an advantageous contract with the city. It is not difficult to see how the victory was brought about. The president of the Royal Electric was J.-B. Thibodeau, a Liberal party stalwart and federal senator. The company's most active partisan in the city council was a Liberal member in the Legislative Assembly, Raymond Préfontaine, formerly mayor of Hochelaga and, in 1886, one of the Hochelaga aldermen in the Montreal city council. Préfontaine was a skilled operator in behalf of the Montreal Street Railway (to employ its new name), and he used his talents and experience in securing for the Royal Electric the franchise for the new utility. Montreal got improved street railway service and electric lighting probably at no greater cost than other cities. Until it was prepared to provide these services itself, it had to depend on private enterprise, which charged what the traffic would bear.

Entangled with discussions of franchise were those of annexation. The term has a sinister sound, but, historically, it meant no more than the free union of bordering municipalities with Montreal. To a striking degree, the fortunes of two of the suburbs affected those of Montreal.[5] They were Hochelaga and St. Jean Baptiste village. Hochelaga was on the St. Lawrence shore east of Montreal, 'a beautiful village'. This aspect diminished when Hochelaga attracted the City Passenger Railway, the Hudon cotton mill, and the North Shore Railway. St. Jean Baptiste village centred on the quarries north of Montreal. In the 1870's, both Hochelaga and St. Jean Baptiste were brought into the Montreal orbit. A decade later, both were annexed to Montreal, Hochelaga in 1883, St. Jean Baptiste in 1885. They became wards of the city and were represented, as the other wards were, by three councillors on the city council. Since five of the six new councillors were French Canadians, they tipped the scales, giving French Canadians a majority on the city council of Montreal. Up to this point, English-speaking councillors seem to have been slightly in the majority. High quality as well as numbers was added: the new wards provided Montreal with two mayors, J.-O. Villeneuve, formerly of St. Jean Baptiste, and Raymond Préfontaine of Hochelaga. Two years after the annexation of St. Jean Baptiste village, the town of St. Gabriel, in the west, was annexed (1887). It was a centre of heavy industry and was drawn increasingly toward Montreal, the Grand Trunk Railway and the Lachine Canal providing the connections. The annexation of these suburbs established a firm precedent. (See Chapter 14.)

The annexations between 1883 and 1887 also constitute the great divide in Montreal municipal history. They brought blocs of new citizens to the city and new leadership to the council. The forces acted on each other. In the old city, by this time, the proportion of the population who were property owners had greatly diminished. In the industrial suburbs, however, the proportion was still high, and it was the worker-owners who were drilled and manipulated to secure the electoral triumphs of their leaders. In this way, Montreal was made ready for Raymond Préfontaine.

RAYMOND PRÉFONTAINE

The civic career of Raymond Préfontaine effectively summarized the post-Confederation age. He was born of farming stock, in 1850, at Longueuil. In his origins he represented the "new Montrealer," the outsider, who was to contribute so materially to the late nineteenth-century city. Préfontaine received his education in Montreal, initially at the hands of the Jesuits at St. Mary's College; later, in the law faculty of McGill University. He practised law in Hochelaga and scored his first civic successes there. He became a member of the town council; later, mayor. It was during his mayoralty of Hochelaga that annexation with Montreal was secured. Préfontaine then became one of the three Hochelaga representatives on the Montreal council. He was the leader in various reform and progressive causes: he secured the abolition of the statute of labour tax, a hoary survival from the eighteenth century; he favoured the enfranchisement of women who were property-holders, a most forward-looking view at that time; and he was instrumental in bringing on the electrification of the street railway. A realist in politics, Préfontaine's ladder to leadership was through the chairmanship of the roads' committee of the city council. It had a large pay roll and awarded many contracts. Long before he became mayor for the first time in 1898, he was the real master of the Montreal administration.

Préfontaine was mayor for three terms, 1898-1901. He personified the French-Canadian ascendancy, not only in city government but throughout Montreal. It was a measure of his magnanimity that in 1902 he refused to stand again, believing that the English population should nominate the mayoralty candidate. Préfontaine had a distinguished public career outside Montreal. He was a member of the Quebec legislature and, later, of the federal parliament. He became a cabinet minister under Sir Wilfrid Laurier. Préfontaine's premature death in 1905 (he was only fifty-five) was a loss that Montreal and Canada could ill afford.

12 TRANSPORT, COMMUNICATIONS, POWER

Urban transportation has something in common with Montreal weather: it is a subject for conversation. It was so at Confederation, and twenty years later its inadequacies figured in the evidence laid before the Royal Commission on Labour. The persistence of complaint underscores the importance of transportation, and of the allied topics of communications and power, in a growing metropolis.

THE LACHINE RAIL-ROAD

Part of Montreal was served by a transportation system as early as 1847. This was a privately owned steam railway, the Lachine Rail-Road, which ran from Windsor and Bonaventure (St. James) streets in Montreal southwest to the town of Lachine.[1] Its real purpose was to transfer freight and passengers to the river steamers that came down to Lachine. However, since there were a number of villages along the route —the Tanneries, Vinet's, Rockfield, and others—the railway enjoyed a great deal of local patronage.[2] It served, in effect, as a suburban line for mass transit, and, given imaginative management, might have become a valuable asset to growing Montreal, comparable to the Paris district railway or the London Metropolitan. In 1864, however, the Lachine railway passed under the control of the Grand Trunk, and the suburban service was allowed to wither. Nonetheless, contemporaries believed that even under Grand Trunk direction (or lack of it) the Lachine railway contributed to the western trend of Montreal.

LES PETITS
CHARS

Transportation within the city was provided from 1861 by the City Passenger Railway. It was owned by the proprietors of the Lachine Rail-Road, who, however, made no attempt to integrate their city and suburban lines. The City Passenger Railway adhered faithfully to the urban pattern of Montreal by having its main lines parallel to the river, along Notre Dame and Craig streets. It was not till 1864 that the earliest north-south line was opened, that on St. Lawrence Boulevard. The cars used were either single or double deck and were drawn by horses. The fare was five cents.

The horse cars of the Montreal Street Railway (the new title was adopted in 1886) covered considerable distances. The east-west lines were over six miles in length; the north-south, about four. By 1892, there were four major and two minor east-west lines, and three north-south. The north-south lines climbed stiff gradients; at what cost to the horses must be left to the imagination. The main north-south line was uphill all the way from Craig Street to St. Jean Baptiste village. (On the steepest grades, it was necessary to add helping teams.) This was the most travelled route of the entire system. In winter, buses mounted on sleighs took the place of the street rail cars. Even at the best seasons, movement was extremely slow, scarcely better than a foot's pace. No time schedule was followed, and the operation was made more haphazard by frequent stops to accommodate favoured patrons. A similar lack of order was apparent in the opening of new lines. The Company may have been guided by interested real estate owners, who offered subsidies. In spite of its insufficiencies, by 1888 the Montreal Street Railway carried well over eight and a half million passengers annually.

For more than thirty years (1861-92), Montreal lived in the horse-car age, its expansion limited by the rate at which a horse could walk. During this period, steam was used on the London underground railway and on the New York elevated. A suggestion to speed service on Montreal streets by the use of steam was rejected, when the charter was under discussion in 1860. Though the decision was rescinded in the early 1870's, the City Passenger Railway did not take advantage of the new possibility.

ELECTRIC TRACTION

As early as 1870, in an amendment to the street railway charter, electricity was mentioned as a source of traction. This is the first suggestion of the transforming power that would come some twenty years later. In September 1892, the first electric street car, appropriately named "The Rocket," went into service in Montreal. In the next two years, the entire railway was electrified, the last horse cars being withdrawn in October 1894. In common with virtually all North American electric city railways, the cars drew their power from an overhead wire.

The electric cars produced a revolution. They were able to operate all year round, since in winter powered snow-ploughs kept the tracks clear. With electrification, regular scheduling was undertaken. The ease and speed with which the new cars could negotiate grades encouraged expansion to the north. All these advantages were immediately shown in the numbers of passengers carried. At the end of the first year of electric operation (September 1893), the Montreal Street Railway reported 17,177,952 paid fares.

THE NEW SUBURBS

The ability of the electric cars to travel long distances was capitalized on early. In the 1890's, two companies, the Park and Island Railway and the Montreal Island Belt Line (later the Montreal Terminal) began to seek franchises from the surrounding towns and villages. By 1894, the Park and Island was so far completed as to warrant a trial run, with a cold lunch at Peloquin's Hotel on Rivière des Prairies, on the northern side of the Island of Montreal. The luncheon party was made up of some interesting celebrities, Senator Thibodeau, Dr. George Bradley, president of the Kensington Land Company (a large real estate speculation), and Messrs. Decary, Valois, and Legault, real estate operators from the Dorval and Ste. Anne de Bellevue area. When completed, the Park and Island Railway served communities as widely separated as Sault-au-Récollet and Lachine. The Montreal Island performed a similar service to the east, linking Maisonneuve (then a separate municipality) and Bout de l'Ile. Both railways had entertainment interest: the Park and Island, Belmont Park; the Montreal Terminal, Dominion Park. From 1893, the Canadian Pacific (using steam, not electricity) developed a suburban service westward along Lake St. Louis. Thus, electric traction—with some help from steam—brought within the social and economic orbit of Montreal a circle of communities that were hitherto a full day's journey away by horse and carriage.[3]

THE AUTOMOBILE

As early as 1898, Montreal had its first motor car, an import from the United States, run by steam. It was furnished with a municipal bicycle licence. In 1901, the first gasoline-driven car was brought from France. (This vehicle may be inspected in the Chateau de Ramezay). In 1902, the Province began to license cars. It issued three permits in Montreal at five dollars each. The owner himself had to paint on the number. Automobiles remained for many years a seasonal blessing. Their general use was interdicted by mechanical deficiencies and by complete inability to cope with winter. It was one of the minor ironies of Montreal history that the street railway, by regular snow removal and by sharing the cost of street paving, made a major contribution to its future rival.

COMMUNICATIONS

Electricity, the transforming agent in travel, had been used much earlier in communications. In 1847, Montreal had been connected with Quebec and New York by telegraph. This was only three years after the invention's first trial in the United States. It had proved of great value to the newspaper press and also to business. It brought the latest market quotations to the Board of Trade and later to the Corn Exchange, and was a powerful encouragement to the setting up of the Montreal Stock Exchange. The pioneer Montreal Telegraph Company later merged with other regional companies and that of the Grand Trunk Railway to form the Great North Western Telegraph Company. Just before Confederation, Montreal installed an electric telegraph fire alarm system. It rang church bells nearest the site of the blaze. This was a great advance over the casual earlier method: "The cry of fire was the signal for an uproar throughout the city. . . . The volunteer companies . . . scattered to every point of the compass."

About ten years after Confederation, the telephone also was brought to Montreal. On February 1, 1878, it was subjected to a rigorous test. A number of "scientific and commercial gentlemen" called Ottawa, and the two cities exchanged "bouquets of songs." They gave renditions of "Rule Britannia," "Home Sweet Home," "We Won't Go Home Till Morning," and "God Save the Queen." The feat was accomplished through the facilities of the Montreal Telegraph Company, which obligingly lent the services of its wires and batteries, in order "to exhibit the powers of Professor Bell's telephone." [4] The Montreal-Ottawa experiment must rank among the earliest long-distance telephone calls, and is of great historical interest in that character. The following year, a bed-ridden member of St. Paul's Church had his house connected to the church by telephone and followed the service by this means. In 1880, the Bell Telephone Company began operations in Montreal, and the use of electricity in communications was formalized.

LIGHTING

In 1879, not long after Montreal was introduced to the telephone, it saw its first electric lights. These were used experimentally on parts of St. James Street and on the Champ de Mars. According to W. H. Atherton, this trial was performed by J. I. Craig, a Montrealer of a scientific turn of mind, who had seen similar lighting at the Paris exhibition of 1878 and secured permission from the city council to try the method in Montreal.[5] Towards the end of May 1879, Montreal militia drilled under what would be described today as floodlights. These were arc lamps set up along the north side of the Champ de Mars. *The Canadian Illustrated News* of May 31, 1879, contained a large drawing to mark the event. For midnight Mass on Christmas eve, 1879, electricity illuminated St. Joseph's Church, on Richmond Street. This is said to be its earliest indoor use for lighting in Montreal.

The next year (1880), a much more extensive experiment was made by the Harbour Commission. It illuminated the wharves with electric light and thus made work "as comfortable and as safe as at midday." The electric current was produced by a small steam-driven generator. When the electricity was switched off, "the wharf appeared to be thrown into . . . complete darkness," although the gas lamps were burning with all their power.[6]

Companies to sell electrical equipment or electric current appeared. In 1882, the Phoenix Company was marketing Craig's arc lamps, dynamos, and storage batteries. In 1884 the Royal Electric Company began to sell direct current. Its power station was on William Street, where it maintained a steam generating plant.

By 1886, the Royal Electric Company was said to have forty miles of cable in Montreal.

It was at this time (1886), when the experimental stage was past, that electricity was used to light the Lachine Canal as far west as the St. Gabriel lock. The new marvel was duly illustrated in G. M. Grant's *Picturesque Canada.* Three years later, April 1, 1889, electric lights went on in all the streets of Montreal. Over a thousand lamps were employed; about three-quarters of them were arc lights. They blazed from eight o'clock in the evening till dawn next morning. Everyone was deeply impressed, although traditionalists complained that the unnaturally bright lights were painful to the eyes. Sweeping claims were made concerning the improvement in morals and the diminution in crime that would certainly follow.

It was not only Montreal that was electrically illuminated. Between 1887 and 1890, the smaller surrounding communities, Ste-Cunégonde, St-Henri, and Côte St-Antoine (Westmount) gave contracts to J. I. Craig, who in 1885 had taken over and extended the services of the Phoenix Company.

POWER

Direct electric current had brought wonders to Montreal—the telegraph in 1847 and the telephone and electric lights about 1880. Montrealers had been quick to seize upon the new form of power. The Royal Electric Company's station, set up on William Street in 1884, was in operation only two years after the opening of the pioneer power stations at Battersea in London and Pearl Street in New York. When alternating current opened the door to marvels without end, its advantages, too, were quickly grasped. Royal Electric began to supply alternating current in 1890.

Alternating current could easily be changed in voltage. A very small current at high tension could be sent many miles over wires of moderate size, with little loss of energy. At the distant point, by lowering the voltage, the current could be increased to suit almost any requirement.

Because distance was no longer a limiting factor, cheap water power from far away could be substituted for costly steam generated close at hand. In 1897, the Lachine Hydraulic and Land Company marketed the first hydroelectric power in Montreal. In 1899, additional hydro-power became available from the Montreal and St. Lawrence Light and Power Company over its transmission line from Chambly, sixteen miles distant.

As the world moved forward into the electrical age, Montreal continued to hold a front-line position. This had been recognized as early as 1891, when Montreal was selected as the site of the international electrical exhibition.[7] It was held early in September, the exhibits being housed in the Victoria skating rink. They covered a considerable range, although the majority were, as might be expected from the date, lighting appliances. Thus there were numerous arc lights, intended chiefly for outdoor use, and incandescent lamps for indoors. The chief displayer of the incandescent lamp, the ancestor of the modern electric light bulb, was "the laboratories of Thomas A. Edison." Similarly, there were extensive exhibits of electroplating devices. Electric cable for the transmission of current and even lamp cord were also shown. The trucks and motor of an electric locomotive attracted a great deal of comment. The object appears to have moved on a short piece of track. (The relevance of this exhibit to the electrification of the Montreal Street Railway scarcely needs stressing.) Finally, a small range of electric tools was shown, precision drills, cutting tools, and so on. These, along with some motors, were forecasts of the industrial electrical age.

The exhibition represented a total effort on the part of Montreal. A number of Montreal manufacturers had displays. These were chiefly electrical appliances or accessories. The current used was provided by the Royal Electric Company and by McGill University, from the generators in its engineering building. Professor John Bovey oversaw the laying of the cable between the university and the Victoria rink. Later, he kept a

close eye on the exhibits and on the visiting public—
to see that the curious were not harmed by examining
too closely. Less conspicuous was Albert J. Corriveau,
the organizer of the electrical exhibition. Corriveau was
a man of the greatest originality. This was supported
by an excellent knowledge of science and mechanical
techniques. His first venture was in the manufacture of
silk. He turned from that to electricity and was one of
the pioneers in introducing it to Montreal. In the early
1890's, he was the force behind many projects for
developing current and using it in light industry. Later,
he would appear as a promoter of electrical railways,
especially of the interurban type. Finally, Corriveau was
to make a place for himself as a pioneer automobile
salesman. He personified the experimenting, questing
spirit that was to mean so much to Montreal in the
new century.[8]

13 THE ERA OF CONSOLIDATION

It is very striking how quickly the impact of the new West and of the transcontinental railway was felt in Montreal. By the end of the 1880's, Montreal was the centre for cattle export, principally from Manitoba and the Northwest Territories (modern Alberta and Saskatchewan) to the United Kingdom. (Tradition states that the trade began in 1860 with two black French-Canadian cows.) In the 1890's, the shipments took on large proportions (netting about $10,000,000 a year), and figured prominently in annual reviews of Montreal business.[1] The animals were brought by train from the prairies, fattened on Quebec and Ontario farms, transferred, again by rail, to Montreal, and shipped live. The same decade witnessed the movement of ever-increasing quantities of western wheat. It was brought by vessel from Fort William to Prescott, stored in elevators, and then moved over the Canadian Pacific line to dockside in eastern Montreal. Here, in the neighbourhood of the modern Jacques Cartier Bridge, the Canadian Pacific Railway had constructed twin elevators, adjacent to the dock and its own marshalling yards (which had formerly belonged to the QMO&O). Being land-based, these elevators were much larger than the small floating ones of earlier times. They were in use in 1888.

To enjoy the benefits of western exploitation fully, Montreal business had to undergo considerable rebuilding. Additional capital and decisive management were requisites. Their provision ushered in the era of the monopoly, and of its instrument, the trust.

EARLY MERGERS

The earliest combination was in the field of power supply. By the end of the century, electricity had become the preferred power in industry, and it was beginning to invade dwellings. In the late summer of

1900, Amy Redpath noted, "The electric people started to-day wiring the house. Top storey in a state of upheaval." Electricity had been produced on a commercial scale since 1884 (see Chapter 12), but its first large-scale industrial use came in 1899, when the Dominion Cotton Mills were electrified and the steam plant abandoned. Two years later, the new Angus shops of the Canadian Pacific employed electricity. However, gas was still used to some extent in industry, and it had considerable sale for domestic purposes, partly for lighting, but especially for cooking. The combining of the Montreal Gas Company with three electrical companies, which had competed not only with gas but with one another, produced an organization that dominated the entire field of power for over forty years. This was the Montreal Light, Heat and Power Company, incorporated in 1901. (In 1916, the term "Consolidated" replaced that of "Company" in the title.)

The electricity and gas monopoly was secured through the merging of the interests of Sir Louis-Joseph Forget and those of Sir Herbert Holt. Forget's chief concern was electricity; Holt's, gas. They might appear to be unlikely allies. Forget (along with his nephew Rodolphe) was from Terrebonne, then a village north of Montreal. He was a financial organizer of great daring and originality, quick to discern new opportunities and to capitalize on them. Holt was an Irishman. He had been an engineer with the Canadian Pacific, but after 1886 had become engaged in financial operations in Montreal. Probably no other two men more shaped modern Montreal, and, by attraction or repulsion, influenced its thinking. Holt survived until 1941, far beyond the period considered in this chapter. His death marked the end of an era: three years later, the Montreal Light, Heat and Power was nationalized.

Both Holt and Forget had other interests. Forget, for example, was president of the Street Railway Company. This corporation secured control over the Park and Island and Montreal Island (Montreal Terminal) railways. With the spread of population, these suburban electric railways later came to be street railways in the ordinary sense of the term.[2] By 1907, the Montreal Street Railway enjoyed a monopoly of transportation in

Montreal and its suburbs. It served both the quick and the dead. For some of the quick, the street railway provided a Black Maria, which carried one-way traffic between the old Court House in Notre Dame Street and the new prison at Bordeaux (opened for business in 1910). For the dead, there was a funeral car—later, cars. These vehicles, discreetly painted in black and gold, gave Montrealers what may be described as the ultimate service.[3]

The essential public services of the municipality, power and transportation, were thus in non-competitive, private hands. Communications, as represented by the telephone, were likewise a private monopoly—that of the Bell Telephone Company. Other industrial activities followed the course to merger or combination. The year 1911 appears to have been a vintage one. *The Canadian Annual Review* listed no fewer than ten mergers in Montreal. They extended all the way from the manufacture of silk to the operation of inland shipping. In several instances, the merger pretty well monopolized production. The merging of two Montreal shoe manufacturers, Ames-Holden and McCready, put D. Lorne McGibbon (of Canadian Felts and Montreal Rubber) "in control of the footwear business of Canada." In other instances, two or more large organizations, by specializing in different forms of the product, shared in the exploitation of the market. For example, the early established McDonald Tobacco and the Imperial Tobacco Company, a recent combine achieved by Sir Mortimer Davis, divided the tobacco market between them.

It might be said that banking followed a line of accommodation, if not of combination. In 1906-7, the Royal Bank of Canada (of which Holt became a director in 1905 and president in 1908) established its main offices in Montreal.[4] It continued to cultivate its Maritime provinces and Caribbean markets—acquired when it was known (before 1900) as the Merchants' Bank of Halifax—and began to develop a new market in the United States. Though located in Montreal, it did not seriously conflict with the old-established Bank of Montreal, whose interests were largely in central Canada. Well before the outbreak of the First World

War, the pattern of development was set, not only in utilities but in other lines of economic endeavour.

The business consolidations of the early twentieth century required capital and familiarity in the manipulation of capital. Experience with the latter was supplied by an institution that long antedated the age of consolidation, the Montreal Stock Exchange. The Exchange, the first of its kind in Canada, had been organized under that name in 1872 and had been incorporated in 1874.[5] Even at that date, trading in securities was ancient history. As early as the 1850's, Montreal newspapers regularly listed stock market quotations. A board of brokers had been set up in 1863. It was from this body that the Montreal Stock Exchange grew.

MAX AITKEN
IN MONTREAL

An early associate of Forget and Holt was Max Aitken, later Lord Beaverbrook. He descended on Montreal in 1907, fresh from financial triumphs in his native Maritimes, where he sold bonds through his Royal Securities Corporation. He transferred this company to Montreal. In his little volume of reflections, entitled *Success,* Aitken inserted those aspects of his Montreal career that he wished to be remembered, his perspicacity, moral courage, and so on. Considering less subjective appraisals as well, other factors emerge. His particular talents were valued by the more adventurous members of the Montreal financial world. The most appreciative appears to have been Sir Edward Clouston, president of the Bank of Montreal, who either suggested or made possible two of Aitken's most spectacular coups, the formation of the Steel Company of Canada and the formation of Canada Cement.[6] In the instance of the former, Aitken transformed what had been first a family business and then a small joint-stock company into one of the largest of Canadian industrial combinations. In the summer of

1910, he left Montreal for even more promising fields in the United Kingdom, travelling to New York, according to his own statement, in an automobile "as big as a house."

Aitken returned briefly to Montreal in the summer of 1912. He then engineered two highly advantageous moves. One was described as the largest real estate deal up to that time—the sale of the so-called High School of Montreal estate, the piece of property on which the Mount Royal Hotel now stands. The other was the initiation of two hydroelectric power schemes in the Montreal neighbourhood, the Long Sault Development and Eastern Canada Power companies. Two years before, Aitken had confessed that he felt "something of an Ishmaelite" in Montreal. Apparently he was made to feel the same again in 1912, and Montreal was left to conduct its affairs without his compelling assistance.

Aitken, however, nourished no grudges. So much is clear in the rather garrulous "My Early Years," published in 1964.[7] He had no cause to, since by his own account, Montreal raised his fortune from about $700,000 to over five million. Moreover, Montreal gave him the taste for what was to be his later, life-long preoccupation—publicity. Nothing daunted by the failure of his Montreal pioneer publishing venture, a weekly, *Canadian Century,* he manoeuvred to control the three English-language dailies, *Herald, Gazette,* and *Star.* The financial difficulties of the *Herald* made it vulnerable. The proprietor accepted a loan of $150,000, and was able to start again after the disastrous fire of June 1910. The *Herald* gave support to policies Aitken had at heart, defeat of reciprocity with the United States and direct contribution by Canada of money to the British navy. *The Gazette* and the *Star* were tougher nuts to crack: Aitken asserted that he was on the point of securing *The Gazette,* when the Canadian Pacific, whose consent (along with that of the Bank of Montreal) had to be obtained in making a transfer of *Gazette* stock, refused. Negotiations with the *Star* were spun out between 1910 and 1912. In November 1912, however, Sir Hugh Graham declined to sell. It is probable that this decision had something to do with

Aitken's determination to quit Montreal. Even fifty years later, he could write, "What might have been my future if *The Montreal Gazette* and the *Herald* had come under my control!"

THE
CAPTIVE
PRESS

Persistent efforts were made to bring about combination in newspaper publishing, sometimes with success. Costs were driving to the wall the old-fashioned individually owned, or party-orientated kind. The pace set by Berthiaume's *La Presse* and Graham's *Star* was breathless, especially when the former increased efficiency by the employment of a research staff and reporters who specialized. In the spring of 1899, *La Minerve* finally suspended publication (see Chapter 8).

La Patrie almost lost its independence. It was the organ of the brilliant, if erratic, Israel Tarte, and was conducted on highly personal lines, in which the opinions of the editor provided the policy of the newspaper. *La Patrie* was Liberal, or, rather, it proclaimed Tarte's version of the official Liberal line. In 1907 Tarte died, at the very moment when, it was believed, the fortunes of *La Patrie* were seriously embarrassed. His sons, Eugène and Louis-Joseph, accepted a loan proffered by Hugh Graham, the proprietor of the *Montreal Daily Star* [8] and agreed to the appointment of his nominees to their board. The nominees, however, soon retired, leaving the sons in possession of the newspaper.

La Presse itself slipped temporarily from Berthiaume's ownership, 1904-6, although not as the consequence of a merger. Its control was secured by an agent of Sir William Mackenzie and Sir Donald Mann, as an element in their involved Montreal strategy for bringing the Canadian Northern Railway into Montreal.

The English-language press shared the disabilities common to both French and English papers and suffered the further one of a comparatively small constituency. The scramble for advertisers and subscribers was very keen indeed. Two old-established newspapers, the *Montreal Herald* and the *Daily Witness,* encountered increasing difficulties.

In June 1910, the *Herald* experienced a disastrous fire in its offices and plant. Although there was no serious interruption in publication, the fire marked the beginning of a period of instability, in which the paper changed hands several times. The changes were certainly connected with dissensions within the Liberal party, of which the *Herald* was a traditional supporter. For about a year, 1913-14, the ownership appears to have been under no political domination whatsoever, but late in 1914 it was once more under Liberal control. Political support and Beaverbrook's loan enabled the *Herald* to escape the clutches of the *Star* in this emergency, and for another thirty years.

The *Witness,* by contrast, was independent in politics, though it had a discernible Liberal bias. To put it another way, it was open to the influence of Sir Wilfrid Laurier. Independence was not a rewarding virtue in the age of big business, and the *Witness* declined— along with its old constituency, the Anglo-Protestant middle class. As early as 1910, it was said that the *Witness* had passed under the control of Graham. Be this as it may, three years later the *Witness* ceased publication. Even in its later, unprosperous days, the *Witness* had been a journalistic training school of very high order. Men of the calibre of John Bassett had formed the staff. Bassett, however, went over to *The Gazette,* perhaps foreseeing the sinking of the ship. He began as *The Gazette*'s parliamentary reporter. He was to rise to the vice-presidency of the company. *The Gazette* possessed a very strong staff—doubtless the chief element in its survival.

In contrast to this chronicle of decay, was the experience of the *Montreal Daily Star.* Hugh Graham's judicious blending of the sensational and the patriotic (or imperial), as described in Chapter 8, carried the *Star* forward. The proprietor rose at the same time. His knighthood was awarded in recognition of his 'extraordinary initiative and zeal . . . [in] safeguarding imperial interests'. Graham's imperial leaning was turned to his own profit and that of Montrealers generally, by his collaboration, about 1903, with John Ross Robertson of the Toronto *Evening Telegram,* to arrange daily cable service of news from Great Britain. Before that time, the only regular news from the United Kingdom was the very scanty offering that came via the United States Associated Press. The format of the *Star* was strikingly modern: the headlines; the signed article; even a rudimentary comic strip, "S'Matter Pop?" By 1914, the cartoons of Racey were an established feature, and, however crude, were always topical. If the *Star* did not offer much to the mind, it certainly catered to the eye. Besides the daily paper, Graham's company published three periodicals: the *Family Herald,* the *Weekly Star,* and the *Standard.* He was credited with even wider ambitions. In 1913, a morning paper the *Daily News*—reputedly Graham's—made its appearance; its vice-president and editor was a former Star employee. The assistance proffered to *La Patrie* was generally interpreted as an attempt to secure an entrée into French-Canadian journalism. Both the *Herald* and *The Gazette* felt impelled at various times to deny that they had passed under *Star* control.

Among English newspapers especially, success in the struggle for survival depended in large measure upon their relation to Canadian Press Limited (known later as The Canadian Press). This co-operative news distributing agency, set up for all Canadian newspapers in 1910, came to be a powerful regulating force. New members (papers not in existence in 1910) were admitted only by vote of the members of the organization. For example, the *Daily News* mentioned above was unable to get a franchise, in spite of the fact that there was only one other English-language morning paper—*The Gazette.* Yet access to the services of Canadian Press Limited was vital, since it had an exclusive contract with the United States Associated Press for sale of its news in Canada. The ownership of the franchises held by the *Witness* and the *Herald* was a matter of absorbing interest, when the demise of those journals became predictable. Graham was accused by *The Gazette* of hastening the end, by cornering the available newsprint supply.

The western unit of the future Canadian Press Limited had been organized in 1907, to battle the company then holding the Associated Press contract—Canadian Pacific Telegraphs, whose rates (for papers in the West) had become exorbitant. In the course of the battle, the federal Railway Commission assumed authority over the rates charged by all telegraph systems, and Canadian Pacific Telegraphs willingly surrendered its contract with the Associated Press. Thereupon, the Canadian newspapers established their own combination—decently disguised as a co-operative—and took up the contract.

It was on this world of merger and combination that Henri Bourassa launched *Le Devoir.* This simple act of faith was, itself, arresting. *"Le Devoir,"* wrote Bourassa, "n'a aucune attache politique ou financière." [9] Here was a declaration of independence that other Montreal newspapers might well envy. *Le Devoir* had the advantage of Bourassa's incisive mind and pen. The intellectual and literary excellence of *Le Devoir* rapidly made it one of the most influential newspapers published in Montreal—possibly in all Canada. It was widely read by the rising French-Canadian middle class (devoutly Roman Catholic, earnest, and public-spirited) and by those Anglo-Canadians who did not mind being shown themselves as Henri Bourassa saw them. Independent; disinterested; honest; *Le Devoir* was a valued supporter of many worthy causes, not least, municipal reform. However, it veered from the championing of social and economic justice to a sterile French-Canadian nationalism.

Les trustards, as the monopolists were called, won all along the line. They maintained a commendable degree of harmony among themselves. They sat on each other's boards. They formed interlocking directorates. They paid lip-service to the principle of competition; but they practised a division of interest. Only once was there a serious quarrel. In the autumn of 1910, J. W. McConnell gained control of the Montreal Street Railway. McConnell was a new star in the firmament. Although he had been a resident of Montreal since 1901, it was only recently that he had entered the adventurous field of company promotion. McConnell was destined to touch Montreal life at many points in the years to come. For the moment, it was enough that he had outmanoeuvred the Forgets and installed his ally Gérald Robert as president of the street railway. A new corporate name was provided, the Montreal Tramways and Power Company. As the last part of the title suggested, the organization was prepared to supply electricity to industrial and domestic consumers. It did so for about fourteen years, from 1910 to 1924, when the power facilities were absorbed by the Montreal Light, Heat and Power.[10]

There was little effective protest. Once (in 1904-5) there was a mild flurry of interest in public ownership of electrical production and supply. No leader was forthcoming to drive home the campaign. One man, indeed, with wider support, might have accomplished much. This was Hormisdas Laporte, the mayor. He was a self-made, self-educated man, in the best sense of those terms.[11] Laporte had made his way unaided, and in honest trade. He was known to be favourable to the principle of public ownership. However, something more robust than general interest was needed to fight the monopoly, with its allies the banks, and its apologist the press. Montreal produced no Adam Beck, and its failure, in view of the talent to hand, is a commentary on its stunted civic sense. In 1915, a municipally owned electrical generating plant was considered, the power to be secured from the aqueduct. Nothing was done till 1944, when the province took over the Montreal Light, Heat and Power. The reign of the monopolists was long and very complete. In the classical life cycle, the Montrealer was born in a house made with Aitken's cement, was surfeited on McConnell's or Redpath's sugar, travelled on Forget's streetcar, paid his bills to Holt's electrical and gas company, smoked McDonald's (Macdonald's) tobacco and Davis's cigarettes, and was buried in a coffin from the casket trust.

14 THE EARLY TWENTIETH CENTURY

The early twentieth century witnessed economic growth such as Canada had not yet seen and Montreal only dreamed of. The period began about 1896, when with the rise in wheat prices the prairie west became an asset of immense value. The discovery of gold in the Yukon in 1897 and 1898 added the enticement of speculation. In 1903, the federal government initiated a railway-building program designed to further national growth. Two years later, in 1905, the new provinces of Saskatchewan and Alberta were created, in order, as Sir Wilfrid Laurier the Prime Minister said, to place the stamp of Canadian nationality on the developing area. This period also saw the first demonstrations of the practicability of air travel: the initial flights of the Wright brothers at Kitty Hawk in 1903; the first Canadian flights, by McCurdy's and Alexander Graham Bell's *Silver Dart,* at Baddeck, on the Bras d'Or lakes, in 1909.

The boom period continued, with certain fluctuations and perhaps with decreasing momentum, until 1913 or 1914. Chapter 13 described the change that Montreal business underwent in this period. What was the human and physical make-up and what was the social and civic development of Montreal under the molding influences of general prosperity, scientific advance, and big business? How did Montreal stand on the threshold of what was optimistically denominated as "Canada's century"?

MONTREAL
AIR MEETS
1906 AND 1910

On July 12, 1906, a primitive dirigible, powered by a motorcycle engine, flew above Dominion Park. This was not the first ascension by a lighter-than-air device at Montreal: fire-balloons (on the Montgolfier principle) had been sent aloft in 1820; and in 1879, a gas-filled balloon carrying two passengers had risen over the city. What made the 1906 performance memorable was that it was the first Canadian powered flight.

At the meet four years later, 1910, although airships were present, attention was centred on aeroplanes. The locale was Lakeside, in modern Pointe Claire; the meet, the largest yet held in America. The cynosure was the Blériot plane *Scarabée,* already famous as the second one to fly the English Channel. It was piloted by Count Jacques de Lesseps. Among other feats, Lesseps engaged in a cross-country flight, in the course of which he circled Montreal and covered thirty-five miles in forty-nine minutes. These were records for both distance and speed. The meet drew vast numbers of spectators, who were carried on the suburban trains of the Canadian Pacific and Grand Trunk railways. On the last day of the meet, July 10, the *Daily Witness* sponsored a model aeroplane contest for Montreal children.[1]

POPULATION
GROWTH

Between 1901 and 1921, population more than doubled, rising from 268,000 (in round figures) to over 618,000. The numbers cited are for the city of Montreal only; had the entire metropolitan area been considered, the total would have been much more imposing. The sharpest increase occurred before 1914 or 1915. In 1911 the city had 470,480 inhabitants; in 1914, an estimated 596,600. The war years produced contradictions: immigration from abroad virtually ceased, but there was a steady inflow from other parts of Canada and from the United States. These newcomers were attracted by Montreal's wartime activities, its industries and its accelerated transportation services.

The proportion of one element of the population remained markedly consistent. French Canadians formed almost 61 per cent of Montreal's people in 1901 and just over 63 per cent in 1921. The actual numbers were 163,016 and 390,168 respectively. On the other hand, Anglo-Canadians, persons of British origin, as the census described them, experienced a reverse. In 1901, they were a full third (33.6 per cent). Twenty years later, they were less than a quarter (24 per cent). Their totals were 90,032 and 148,630 respectively. Persons who were neither French nor British by origin made impressive gains. In 1901 they formed only 5 per cent of the population; in 1921, 12.8 per cent. At that date, they had reached over half the strength of the English. The trends observable by the early 1920's were to persist. The French Canadian had established complete predominance. The Anglo-Canadian position continued to slip, in spite of the shoring-up provided by British immigration both before and after the war.[2] The non-French, non-English group was coming into its own.

Of this last group, only the Jews and the Italians were numerically significant. The Jews were strengthened by new arrivals from what had been the Austro-Hungarian Empire, from Poland (formerly a Russian province), and, increasingly, from Rumania.[3] Charitable and educational agencies were put under great strain. The answer was their amalgamation in 1914 into the Federation of Jewish Philanthropies. The success of the Federation was an object lesson to other groups, which, like the Jews, experienced the loss of homogeneity and the disappearance of a well-defined area of settlement. The Italians retained cohesion through their common language and their church organizations. Canon Bruchési's mission (see Chapter 10) became a parish in 1905—Our Lady of Mount Carmel. A second parish, Our Lady of Defence, was set up in 1911.

The great new population (of whatever origin) helped to upset the old pattern of concentration. The most densely settled parts of the city, heretofore in the south and the centre, became the northeast and the east. Numerically, the largest wards were Laurier, Mercier, and St-Denis, with populations up to forty thousand. No other ward could equal this figure, although in 1921 St-Henri approached it with a population of over thirty thousand. It was evident that the big battalions were to be found in the working-class wards. Only gradually did they become conscious of their strength; perhaps it was not till the election of Médéric Martin as mayor in 1914 that there was a clear declaration of where political power lay.

THE
MOVEMENT
UPTOWN

"The movement uptown of trade to St. Catherine Street has continued and now such firms as . . . Morgan, Murphy, Ogilvy, Birks, Notman, Hamilton, Tooke, Dickson, Cassidy, and Holland are to be found in that fast-improving street. . . . The Bell Telephone Company . . . have laid their wires underground. . . . The Lachine Hydroelectric Power Company have followed their example." Thus wrote the editors of Lovell's Directory. The year was 1896, when the Directory itself had passed its half-century mark of utility to Montrealers.[4] An omission from this honour roll of historic retail merchant names is that of Dupuis Frères. Though second in age only to Morgan's, this store had been established from the first on the upper level. In the figurative sense too, Montreal had gained the rim of a plateau of fresh development. The new pattern of urban expansion that was taking shape would remain valid for at least a quarter of a century; certainly till the end of the First World War. Even seventy years after the Lovell editors wrote, three of the great houses referred to (Morgan, Ogilvy, and Birks), and Dupuis as well, are still operating under the same names and on the same sites as in 1896.[5]

EXPANSION
NORTH AND EAST

"The movement uptown" was only a small part of the enormous drift of industry and population. The general direction was north and east. An observer on the eastern crest of Mount Royal could not fail to be struck by the rapid growth of the city below him: streets being laid; buildings rising from the fields and woods of an earlier time. The ascent of the mountain was no longer the breath-taking exercise it had been. In 1886, the Mountain Elevator, or incline railway, was opened. This "marvel of science," consisting of two counter-balanced, cable-drawn cars, climbed from Fletcher's Field to the crest of the mountain.[6]

The electric street railway now completely circled Mount Royal. It was one of the forces making possible the new growth. The other was large-scale real estate development. Lines were rapidly being built across the easy levels north and east of the City Passenger Railway's old terminus at Hochelaga, an area in which the operation of the second force could be easily seen. In 1883, following the annexation of Hochelaga, a new municipality on its east boundary—Maisonneuve— was incorporated. The founding fathers were six or seven land speculators, who laid out a modest suburb, giving due attention to (along with their own profits) water supply, street planning, and primitive zoning regulations.[7] Farther inland, Rosemount was another real estate developers' creation. In this, astute advantage was taken of the Canadian Pacific's great Angus shops. Sometimes the railway and the realty operator joined hands. The Park and Island Railway and the Kensington Land Development Company appear to have united to exploit Notre Dame de Grâce West, the area of modern Girouard Avenue.

Roads, railways, and, above all, electric railways provided the net for this seemingly random expansion. Local land booms were carefully engineered, and back-country villages and obscure crossroads found themselves suddenly elevated into urban communities. What was wanting was over-all planning; private enterprise and the profit motive were poor substitutes. As a result of this lack, Montreal found itself the centre of an extraordinarily confused and complex peripheral growth. Confusion was compounded by conflicting municipal jurisdictions and ambitions. The simple appetites of the one-big-city enthusiasts, who sought wholesale annexations, were thwarted by suburban administrations, bent on maintaining local autonomy. By 1903 or 1904, something of a crisis was reached.

MAJOR ANNEXATIONS
STE-CUNÉGONDE
ST-HENRI
MAISONNEUVE

Outside the municipal boundaries of Montreal but indistinguishable from it, were the industrial cities of St-Henri and Ste-Cunégonde. St-Henri, indeed, was described as the third city in Quebec, with a population of nearly twenty-two thousand.[8] Ste-Cunégonde was about half that size. Both cities lay along the Grand Trunk Railway and the Lachine Canal. Their industries were leather-working (hence the historic significance of the name St-Henri des Tanneries), cloth-manufacturing, and, in the instance of Ste-Cunégonde, heavy industry. So completely were they parts of Montreal that Lovell included them in the Montreal street-listings. In 1905, both Ste-Cunégonde and St-Henri were annexed to Montreal. At the same time, and with little geographical logic, the village of Villeray, which lay to the northeast, was annexed as well. Between 1905 and 1919 no fewer than nine municipalities were absorbed: six in 1909 and 1910; three between 1916 and 1919. By a curious turn of fate, the last to be annexed, the city of Maisonneuve, owed its origin to the first of all the annexations, that of Hochelaga.

WESTMOUNT
OUTREMONT

This was not the whole story. Six municipalities remained outside—an ambiguous description, since two at least were virtually surrounded by Montreal. The two were Westmount and Outremont. Under the prettier designation of Côte St-Antoine, Westmount had been incorporated in 1879.[9] At that time it lay along Côte St-Antoine Road, which climbs the western shoulder of Mount Royal towards Notre Dame de Grâce. "Its inhabitants," wrote a contemporary, "are chiefly merchants doing business in Montreal." Less than twenty years later, Westmount (the name was made official in 1894) had a population of about ten thousand. "The electric cars afforded rapid communication with Montreal." Westmount cherished its autonomy, and in consequence it was able to engage in some interesting municipal projects, for example the production of electricity. In April 1906, Westmount made the first municipally generated electricity in Quebec.[10] Outremont (1875) belonged to the same period in organization. It occupied an indefinite area on the northern slopes of Mount Royal. The coming of the street railway along Côte Ste. Catherine Road had been all that was necessary to open the large landholdings of the Wiseman and Beaubien families.

VERDUN
LACHINE
MONTREAL WEST
ST-LAURENT

The four remaining towns, Verdun, Lachine, Montreal West, and St-Laurent, were more widely separated and boasted distinctive histories. Verdun and Lachine were river towns west of Montreal. An early figure of significance in Verdun was John Crawford, a land speculator and power in the City Passenger Railway, a familiar combination. Early settlers might be described as refugees from Pointe St. Charles, that traditionally neglected part of Montreal.[11] The nearness of heavy industry in St. Gabriel and at Côte St. Paul doubtless served as a positive attraction. Lachine too was supported by heavy industry. The building of the Canadian Pacific's bridge across the St. Lawrence in 1886 may be taken as the beginning of modern Lachine. The locating there of the Dominion Bridge Company and other metal works strengthened the new direction—one that left virtually no reminder of the older Lachines of the fur trade and Lake St. Louis navigation.[12] Montreal West and St-Laurent lay inland. The former was entirely new; it grew up at the junction of the Canadian Pacific's line from the Windsor Station with the one south to the Lachine Bridge (see Chapter 7). St-Laurent, north of the mountain, was at the drawing together of several roads, the chief of which were Côte Vertu and what is now Decarie Boulevard. It was a place of importance as far back as the eighteenth century, but in 1847 it received an entirely new impetus when the Fathers of the Holy Cross established their College. Some fifty years later, the extension of the Park and Island Railway brought St-Laurent into the Montreal orbit.

THE TOWN
OF
MOUNT ROYAL

The operations of the two promotional forces, real estate and railway, got their best exemplification in the Town of Mount Royal. In the estimation of the more ambitious speculators, the Grand Trunk and Canadian Pacific railways, by cutting through both lower and upper levels, had ruined any opportunity for really large-scale land development in southern and western Montreal. Only the north remained, and that, only if it could be made accessible by speedy rail connection. The solution was provided by Mackenzie's and Mann's Canadian Northern Railway, which was seeking entry into central Montreal.[13] The railway's chief engineer, Henry Wicksteed, suggested tunnelling under Mount Royal. This would bring the railway into the heart of the city and provide a route to the flat, open country north of Mount Royal, an area that had hitherto discouraged even the most hardy speculative builders. There followed land deals on a truly imperial scale. The Northern got its Montreal station site between Dorchester Boulevard and St. James Street. Here it planned to construct a grandiose station, head offices, and hotel. The real estate speculators got their land— about 5700 acres—at the northern portal of the connecting tunnel. The tunnel was built between the summer of 1912 and December 1913. On October 21, 1918, the first train from the north entered Montreal.

Between those dates, the new suburb had been laid out. Though its official name is simply "Mount Royal," it is always spoken of as "The Town of Mount Royal." The ground-plan declares its origin: all the main streets radiate from the railway station.

THE EMERGENCE OF A NEW CLASS

Class lines cut across all racial segments of the Montreal population. The well-to-do were remote in their brownstone mansions on Dorchester Boulevard or Sherbrooke Street. They were little inconvenienced by the periodic epidemics that ravaged the crowded tenements of the northeastern wards or of the "city below the hill." In the spring of 1909, an outbreak of typhoid fever paralysed much of the city. The poor struggled with the spiralling prices of the boom years before 1912, and then with the unemployment that came with 1913 and 1914. In all this there was little class hostility, but much indifference and ignorance. The unresolved economic and social problems of the times were illustrated each May Day: six thousand paraders under the red flag denounced in ten languages the enormities of property and police, while thirty-five thousand Montrealers trailed about the streets moving to new homes, the victims of the absurd convention that caused all leases to be renewable on May the first.

Between the extremes of wealth and poverty, a new class was emerging. While there always had been a middle-income group, it lacked the homogeneity and self-consciousness of a class. Whereas thirty years before, clerical workers had been a tiny fraction of the work force, they now formed a body of considerable size. (Clerical staffs were male; it was not till the period of the First World War that women were generally employed in Montreal offices.) Two other elements went into the composition of the new class: some professional men and the better paid foremen and master mechanics. Salaried and black-coated (rather than wage-earning and blue-shirted), the group was cut off financially from the owners above and occupationally from the manual workers below. Such was the Montreal middle class.

It was composed of both French Canadians and Anglo-Canadians. The former were probably the more numerous and rapidly became the more significant. They formed the reading public of *Le Devoir* and fell in easily with the social and political preachments of Henri Bourassa. The English, on the other hand, failed to respond to the *Daily Witness* (in a sense *Le Devoir*'s counterpart), and this failure hastened the demise of that once powerful journal. The French element drew ahead. It was benefited by the great new day schools, such as Academie Mont St-Louis, whose curriculum followed that of the classical colleges. In 1919, the independence of the Montreal division of Laval University was won. A Papal rescript in that year and an act of the legislature in 1920 established the autonomy of the Université de Montréal. Thereafter, French-Canadian Montreal would set its own intellectual measure.

THE
NEW BROOM
AT QUEBEC

In 1905, a palace revolution within the Liberal cabinet brought Lomer Gouin to the premiership of Quebec. He was, possibly, the ablest premier to serve the province. Certainly, he was the only one really appreciative of Montreal. He had roots in the city, and he represented the Montreal constituency of St. James in the legislature (1897-1908). A contemporary newspaper expressed its admiration in these terms: "The change in Premiership would seem to have lifted Quebec from the standards of the bookkeeper to those of the statesman. . . . If the pledges given . . . are any index of what his [Gouin's] course will be . . . Sir Wilfrid Laurier might well forward . . . his unreserved congratulations." For fifteen years (1905-20), Sir Lomer—as Gouin became in 1908—was premier of Quebec. They were years of great progress for the province. If the progress of Montreal was more checkered, the fault was not Sir Lomer Gouin's.

Gouin and his cabinet were deeply concerned with education. In one of his earliest public addresses, Gouin said, "The great political problem is . . . education. . . . It is in the schools that men are formed." This enthusiasm was to the advantage of Montreal. Between 1910 and 1914, the educational range in the city was extended by the opening of the Ecole des Hautes Etudes Commerciales, the Ecole Technique de Montreal, and the Ecole des Beaux Arts. These were provincial government schools of highly specialized character. In 1914, the Montreal Protestant School Commission provided a new home for the High Schools of Montreal. All of these schools are still in use, and their general seemliness and dignity of design suggest the material improvement that had come with the new administration at Quebec.

The universities felt the new impetus through increased endowments. At McGill, the teaching of the physical sciences had been greatly stimulated by the tenure of Ernest Rutherford, later Lord Rutherford, as Professor of Physics (1898-1907). His researches in radiation led to his receiving the Nobel prize for chemistry in 1908, and in 1911 to a postulation of the present theory of the structure of the atom. Professor Frederick Soddy of the chemistry department also made an important contribution to research in radiation.

In 1907, McGill opened Macdonald College at Ste. Anne de Bellevue, to house agriculture, household science, and teacher training. An even more distant project was the affiliation, as junior colleges, of the high schools of Victoria and Vancouver (1899-1902). The latter was known as the McGill University College of British Columbia. This interesting experiment came to an end in 1915, when the provincial University of British Columbia began teaching.

In 1909, the provincial government set up a Royal Commission to conduct an inquiry into Montreal municipal administration. Demands for such an inquiry were long-standing, reaching back, indeed, to the middle 1890's. The initiators then, and the group which succeeded in stirring action in 1909, were "the public bodies," the Chambre de Commerce and the Board of Trade. Initially, the rising cost of city administration had been the main cause of grievance. Letters of protest and delegations of protesters worried the city council and the Quebec legislature. The Private Bills Committee of the legislature was subject to continuous pressure, when measures designed to widen the borrowing powers of the City of Montreal were under examination. Organizations, such as "the Good Government Association," formed in 1895, constituted themselves vigilance committees and multiplied complaints. In the early twentieth century, while charges of waste, extravagance, and peculation were continued, a new and more positive line was entered on: a demand for a thorough overhaul of city government to make it more genuinely representative and efficient.

A great deal of the new driving force was borrowed from the programs of municipal reformers in the United States, and, probably, in Europe. The adjective "progressive" hallowed every cause. The provincial government was open to suggestion. It, too, aspired to be progressive. Sir Lomer Gouin was modern in his point of view. He was nothing if not sympathetic. Gouin was determined to secure honest and efficient government for the province; he could do scarcely less than to secure them for Montreal, whose financial credit and general morale it was so necessary to maintain. The upshot was the appointment of the Royal Commission presided over by Mr. Justice Lawrence John Cannon. The Commission's report, made in 1909, was a devastating indictment of Montreal municipal administration for a decade. It was described as being "saturated with corruption." The root of the evil was clearly indicated: the wide diffusion of authority within the unwieldy council; the power annexed by certain city councillors. They consistently acted together, supporting each other's measures and securing for themselves, or their favourites, the lion's share of contracts and concessions. Eight were named as most guilty.

LE RÉGIME
DES
HONNÊTES GENS

In consequence of the investigation, Montreal was provided with a new form of government. According to the revised charter, a four-man board of control along with the mayor formed the executive. They and he were elected by the city at large; in other words, without reference to the wards. The wards had been little satrapies over which the councillors ruled supreme. They dispensed favours; jobs; privileges; remissions of fines. A thorough reformation would have swept away the wards, but through the legislature's ignorance or inertia they were allowed to stay on. The city council, elected on the ward basis, remained, but was largely shorn of its powers. To describe it as the legislative branch of the new instrument of government is to misuse terms. It was a species of sounding-board of public opinion.

A referendum, the chosen instrument of the progressives, indicated approval of the new form of city government. In the atmosphere of the moment, which resembled a religious revival and recovery following a prolonged debauch, the municipal elections were held. A citizens' association, heavy with representatives of the mercantile and financial oligarchy, prepared a slate of acceptable candidates for board of control and city council. They were supported, in general, by the Société Saint-Jean-Baptiste and by other organizations of the same social stratum. Even the newspapers, which had enjoyed vast increases in sales during the scandal revelations, supported the new régime, dedicated to the elimination of scandal. This administration enlisted the enthusiastic, if temporary, support of Henri Bourassa, then in the throes of launching *Le Devoir*. In the first issue of his new journal, Bourassa proclaimed, "Le Devoir appuiera les honnêtes gens et denoncera les coquins." [14] The new administration, dominated by the board of control, is historically important, because it is the earliest of many means taken to improve city government in Montreal—a recurring pursuit in twentieth-century history.

The rule of the honest men during the next four years was an uneven performance. The cost of administration remained high, and so, therefore, did the taxes. In view of the rapid growth of the city, it is difficult to see how this could have been otherwise. Rising cost, however, did not redound to the credit of a form of administration recommended as being economical. The worst abuses of patronage were eliminated. What were not corrected were the exactions of the great franchise holders, the street railway company, and the electrical power and gas corporation. That the exactions were not corrected was laid increasingly to the board of control itself, whose membership contained men connected with the corporations. Support for municipal reform as exemplified by the board of control ebbed. *Le Devoir* caught the prevailing mood when it grumbled that little men were pilloried for trivial offences, while the rich were allowed to go unexposed and unpunished. The final disaster came in December 1913, when the aqueduct broke, creating a serious water-famine. It was a sad commentary on the efficiency of a municipal service under the rule of the honest men.

15 1914 AND AFTERWARDS

On April 6, 1914, Médéric Martin was elected for the first time mayor of Montreal. He was to repeat this success on four later occasions.[1] However, no one of Martin's later triumphs exceeded in significance his first victory in 1914. It closed one period in Montreal municipal history and opened another. Médéric Martin was the first of "the people's" mayors—people's in the sense that they sought identification with the masses and attempted to govern through their personal popularity. Until his time, the mayors had been drawn from, and spoke for, the commercial oligarchy. True, they might have risen from very humble origins, but they made no effort to exploit their proletarian past—or to advance the interests of their proletarian contemporaries. In the council, it was not thought unbecoming for an alderman to pose as "the people's Jimmy," but the mayor was supposed to be an Olympian. It is one of Martin's claims to recollection that he refused to follow convention. He based much of his career on the fact that he was a poor man's son. As he was fond of saying, he desired to be mayor of *all* Montreal.

Martin was to take office at an awkward moment. The hectic good times of railway construction and real estate and building booms were fading away. For the unskilled and even for the skilled, 1913 and 1914 were, indeed, years of the locust. Nevertheless, Martin was not brought in by economic collapse, or even by social upheaval. Rather, his triumph came through the abdication of the nineteenth-century political nation. The coincidence of economic hardship and the appearance of proletarian leadership is really deceptive. The hard times were to give way to the inflationary prosperity of the First World War. The proletarians were to show themselves incapable of rule.

136

MÉDÉRIC
MARTIN

Médéric Martin was a Montrealer by birth and by lifelong residence. Thus he broke the tradition that had given distinguished newcomers a preferred place in Montreal civic life. Born in 1869, he was in his vigorous middle-forties when he came to the mayoralty contest of 1914. It was held to Martin's discredit by his critics that his formal education was meagre. In reality, it had been carried into secondary school, an unusual height in the working-class world of his boyhood. He had two advantages. Because he grew up in St. Mary's ward (the largest of the thirty-four wards into which Montreal was then divided), he understood instinctively the point of view of his people. Secondly, Martin did not lose touch with his working-class origins. He was a cigar-maker, and to the end of his political career was careful to retain his membership card in Local 58 of the Cigar Makers' Union. Throughout, Martin made shrewd use of these advantages. His claim to be a native son was simon-pure. Was he not just "un autre gars de Ste-Marie"? In his calling as the skilled working man, Martin appealed to that group, and also to a wider group, for whom membership in one of the skilled trades was the peak of ambition. One of the best remembered aspects of the Médéric Martin era was his entertainment of distinguished visitors. The Mayor's handsome features were displayed to advantage beside those of Marshal Joffre, or even of Queen Marie of Rumania. In the most exalted company, Martin did not forget his past, nor those who had made his eminence possible. Surely it was an artist's stroke to present the Prince of Wales, the future Edward VIII, with a large box of cigars made by the Mayor's own hands.[2]

ELECTION
BACKGROUND

Like many other public careers, Martin's had been checkered. It began propitiously in 1906. First, he was elected to the Montreal city council as one of the aldermen from St. Mary's ward. In November of the same year, he was successful in a by-election for the federal House of Commons, also from the constituency of St. Mary's. Martin, therefore, straddled municipal and federal politics and made them a mutually advantageous combination. He was a Liberal, and derived a good deal of reflected glory from his cultivated intimacy with Sir Wilfrid Laurier. At a later time, Martin used to boast that Sir Wilfrid would say playfully that he must have a Mass said for Martin's defeat as mayor of Montreal, so that he could devote his full genius to federal politics. Political realist that he was, Laurier valued Médéric Martin's peculiar talents, and some very worthwhile patronage was made available to the member for St. Mary's.[3] Martin was returned triumphantly at the general elections of 1908 and 1911. The latter was no small achievement, in view of the Liberal rout before the Conservative-Nationalist coalition. Doubtless a careful reading of portents caused him to decline to run in 1917.

Martin's municipal career received a set-back in 1909, as a result of the Cannon Commission inquiry. He was named as one of the eight most guilty councillors and forced to resign his seat. However, as the vested interests continued to thrive under the rule of the honest men, the misdeeds of the little men seemed less heinous. Martin was re-elected to the council in 1912.

In the council he was the head of what was virtually an opposition party and was able to obstruct the legislative program of the board of control. He made good use of his knowledge of parliamentary tactics, acquired in Ottawa, to dominate the city council. Outside, Martin spoke endlessly at public meetings, where his command of the popular argot and his intimate knowledge of the city were of inestimable service. Long before nomination day, he was the people's choice for mayor. In all these preliminaries, there was very little in the way of organization on Martin's part. He had no machine, as the term is usually understood. It is true that there were "workers' clubs" that supported him, but these were small and scattered. There was also the rallying song, "The Martinaise." Neither its air nor inspiration was difficult to trace. Médéric Martin's appeal was a personal one, the little man to the little men.

THE MUNICIPAL ELECTIONS OF 1914

The upholders of the existing régime were in great confusion. This was made the greater by an irrelevant squabble over the mayoralty. The English were sulky, and disposed to insist that it was their turn to nominate the candidate. The last English mayor, Henry A. Ekers, had held office between 1906 and 1908, on the eve, in other words, of the Cannon Royal Commission. In spite of this inauspicious circumstance, the English-language press took up the quarrel. *The Montreal Star* and its satellites, the *Witness* and the *Herald,* used language reminiscent of the high summer of English domination in the 1840's and 1850's. They were provocative and truculent. It is a commentary on the willingness of the political nation to come to agreement that the French-Canadian ruling class accepted the English claim and put up no candidate. In earlier elections, this understanding would have meant complete absence of any serious French-speaking contender. The unreal basis of the alternating mayoralty was exposed in a series of letters in *Le Devoir,* irony of ironies, written in English by Henri Bourassa himself.[4] (Later, the letters were published in pamphlet form.) Starting from the proposition that whatever the English did was wrong, Bourassa had no difficulty in showing how irresponsible their claim to the mayoralty was, constituting as they did not much more than one-third of the city's population. This literary blast had no effect on the decision to nominate an English-speaking candidate, although it may have had on the later electoral campaign. The immediate problem was to find a candidate. To the consternation of the English minority and to the irritation of the French-Canadian majority, none was forthcoming. By way of contrast, there was an overflow of English aspirants for the board of control, in spite of the convention that allowed them only one of the four. It was not until the first week of March that an English candidate for the mayoralty was found. He was George Washington Stephens.

Stephens was the personification of the old political society, crossed with the new financial class. He was the son of "Watch-Dog-of-the-Treasury" Stephens of the 1870's and 1880's, from whom he inherited one fortune. He made another through the manipulation of rubber manufacturing. Stephen's Canadian Rubber Company was a comfortable monopoly, said to embrace every rubber manufacturer in Canada but one. It was formed in the best approved, modern manner, through the control of stock. In politics, Stephens was a Liberal. He had been a member of the Quebec provincial cabinet. More recently, he had been chairman of the Montreal Harbour Board, to which he was appointed by Sir Wilfrid Laurier. The debacle of the federal election of 1911 cost Stephens that post, but made him available for the Montreal mayoralty. As an administrator he had shown ability and imagination.

On Stephens's side, the mayoralty campaign of 1914 had many of the overtones (perhaps unconsciously) of Theodore Roosevelt's presidential campaign of 1912. "My hat is in the ring," prefaced Stephens's declaration of his candidature. He had "come back . . . for the fight." "The Major," as he liked to be called from his peace-time service with the Montreal Field Battery, radiated confidence. Stephens was very modern in his campaign methods. Three telephones were installed in his campaign headquarters. At speaking engagements, he would dazzle his supporters by dramatic arrivals in his automobile. On voting day he assembled a fleet of "motors" to transport the aged or the sedentary to the polls. At the same time, Stephens displayed great political naivety. He produced an elaborate electoral program, calling for the establishment of a public library, and for limitations on the rapacity of the tramways company, to cite only two of its elements. It was much too good to be true, and much too costly to carry out. It paid scant attention to vested interests.

Stephens's platform simply gave gratuitous talking-points to Médéric Martin. He was relieved of developing a platform of his own, and devoted his talents to poking fun at (and holes in) Stephens's. Martin knew his people. He met them constantly at street corners or in dingy, smoke-filled mission halls in the crowded northern and eastern wards and in the "city below the hill." Always, it was his identification with Montreal and its poor, and Stephens's with distant places and with the rich. Médéric Martin did not wage a racial campaign, despite the accusation then, and the repetition of the accusation at later times.

He did not have to, for he completely personified his stratum of French-speaking Montreal as Stephens did his English one. His followers exulted in the prospect of a French-Canadian mayor; of one of the lowly occupying the place of the mighty. And Martin was not without resources. The public utility companies were on his side. Part of their help took the form of hindering his opponent. Stephens complained of lukewarm newspaper support, especially of the English newspapers. It is a fact, also, that Martin was to receive his greatest majorities in such wards as Hochelaga and St-Henri, where the shops and main car-barns of the tramways were situated.[5]

The election was held on April 6, a Monday. It brought out what was described as a record vote, 75,945. In reality, this was only about ten thousand more than had gone to the polls in 1912. Two features of the 1914 election were of interest: virtually all disqualifications had been removed, especially those connected with failure to pay taxes (property taxes of the owners; water taxes of the tenants). A large number of women (property holders) were for the first time eligible to vote. G. W. Stephens had paid special court to the women, addressing meetings sponsored by the

National Council of Women, La Fédération de Saint-Jean-Baptiste, and the Women's Suffrage Association. Female activists, such as Mme Gérin-Lajoie, Dr. Helen Reid-England, and Professor Carrie Derrick of McGill, were given prominent places on Stephens's platforms. On the other hand, Martin was singularly unresponsive. He said that he was married to one woman, and that was enough. It was believed that of the thirteen thousand women eligible, over eight thousand voted. The rival candidates awaited the results in their respective strongholds, Stephens in the editorial offices of *La Presse;* Martin, in the Club canadien. They were not kept long in doubt. Even before the full returns of the big wards came in, Martin was leading by over two thousand. The final count, established two days later, gave Martin 40,753; Stephens, 35,192. "The great voice of the people" enjoyed a majority of 5,561.

As well as giving Montreal a new mayor, the elections of 1914 gave it a new board of control and a new council. The results here were quite as decisive. The civic reformers won only two of the four seats. Perhaps the explanation for the poor showing of the old political nation is contained in this quotation presenting the view of C. C. Ballantyne, Stephens's replacement on the Harbour Commission: "It was difficult to hope for the best men as controllers, since they were . . . handicapped by inadequate pay. . . . In his business a salary of $7,000 would be laughed at." [6] Civic responsibility and the laurel wreath had lost their former appeal. In the council, a majority was prepared to follow Martin. They did not form a party; perhaps they followed him because there was no one else to follow. English-speaking membership on the thirty-one man council shrank to five, or to seven, if the two Jewish members were prepared to range themselves with the minority. The election produced ill-natured recriminations. *Le Devoir* discerned not only "the profound division of race, but [the] conflict of the masses against the classes," which allowed "the victory of a man of the fifth-order." (In the light of frankness such as this, it is not hard to understand why *Le Devoir* was not Médéric Martin's favourite reading.) All critics blamed the apathy of the English electors, who were made the convenient scapegoat to account for a result that no member of the old political nation composed of the commercial oligarchy had foreseen or desired.

AFTERMATH

Martin's most urgent problem was to find jobs. He tried to make work, the city itself becoming the employer. His crude blend of social economics was early deployed: "The money . . . voted . . . for [public] works . . . is to be spent quickly. We want no more of the system whereby a small number of men have been employed for the whole season. We want a large number of men to work for a little while." On the morning of the twentieth, four thousand unemployed swarmed round the city hall in enthusiastic approval. To them the mayor said: "We are going to give work to people as quickly as possible. Today we will take on 2000 men. To-morrow we will have money voted so that the sewer work may commence. . . . I tell you that in eight days there will not be a tax-payer without employment." Despite these brave words, unemployment continued. Finally, Martin was compelled to appeal to Sir Robert Borden, the Prime Minister, thus loading off on the broad back of the federal government the problems for which he could supply no solution.

Martin announced that as mayor he would take an active part in all committee work. As a means of co-ordinating municipal administrative services, this declaration was well received. More ominous, however, was the second announcement—that he would assume complete control of the city's employees and their yearly pay-roll of almost four million dollars (about a third of the city's revenue). Old cronies were well cared for. One of the aldermen "wounded" in the Cannon inquiry was installed as chairman of the public works' committee. In July, in gratitude for past favours, and perhaps in anticipation of future ones, a motley crowd of city officials, contractors, and political hangers-on gathered at Martin's summer house at

Laval-des-Rapides and there presented the hero with $10,000 in gold. The victor was being invited to divide the spoils.

Other problems did not lend themselves to easy solution. The financial position of Montreal was precarious. Martin was unable to raise sufficient money from taxation. Finally, he accepted the inevitable, applied to a group of banks for a loan, and, in return, had to accept their supervision of municipal finances. Transportation remained the most obstinate of all Montreal's difficulties. Someone might have made a puzzle out of it to sell in the streets. The Tramways Company insisted that it could not extend its services without a subsidy or a new contract carrying with it extended privileges. The city, already heavily in debt, could not afford the subsidy; still less could it consider expropriation. A subway or a motor bus service, although widely canvassed, was technically impractical at that time.

The Martin era endured for almost a decade and a half (1914-28). Much more was lost than fourteen or fifteen years. The whole democratic process in municipal administration was placed in jeopardy. The fault was not entirely Médéric Martin's. The real cause of the malady lay in Montreal society itself. The old political nation of the post-Confederation period no longer led. The new political nation that was to be dominant by the centenary of Confederation was not yet capable of leadership. Neither Médéric Martin nor any of the later people's mayors could span the gap.

THE FIRST WORLD WAR

Within five months of Martin's taking office, Montreal was engulfed by the First World War. This was the most devastating event of the fifty years after Confederation. It took a heavy toll of human life, probably heaviest among the rising middle class upon whom the future was so to depend. It is a thought to ponder, the gain Montreal would have experienced had the young lives so generously given to war been devoted to the city's service. The war placed a severe strain on the effective *entente* between French and English, at that time the two major racial groups. The war years found no solution for the continuing problems of finance and transportation. Little wonder that Montreal dragged its pace for almost ten years following the Armistice.

The outbreak of war took Montrealers by surprise— some of them embarrassingly so. Sir Lomer Gouin was summering in Brittany. He was to experience considerable difficulty in getting home. His rival, Henri Bourassa, was taking a busman's holiday in Alsace. There, he was seeking evidence to support the often-made claims that the French Canadians in Ontario were living under greater tyranny than were the Alsatians under Prussia. By dint of hard walking, he made his way across the French border, and so back into Canadian history. One wonders what would have been the effect on M. Bourassa of experiencing in his own person four years of Prussian rule in a German internment camp.

There was widespread sympathy for France. This showed itself in anxious crowds before the bulletin boards of the newspaper offices, and in the singing of "La Marseillaise" on every occasion. French and Belgian reservists were fêted. On August 8, when the first body of French reservists left Montreal, they received an ovation. Four days earlier (August 4), the British declaration of war on Germany had automatically bound Canada to the same course. The response of Montreal was one of enthusiasm, indeed of fervour, which showed how little an unmilitary people understood the reality of war. On August 15, a large public meeting was convoked on the Champ de Mars. The iniquity of Germany was denounced and the determination of Montrealers to prosecute the war fully was vociferously applauded. A march-past of troops followed, the majority of the units wearing the brilliantly coloured uniforms of earlier days. A late summer storm broke over the city as the meeting ended. It was strangely prophetic of Montreal's experience during the next four and a quarter years.

Montreal's war service was cut across by controversy over recruiting, and later, over conscription. Federal policy dictated that the historic militia regiments should not be sent overseas, but should be used as the means of recruiting men for the Canadian expeditionary forces.[7] Those members who volunteered were formed into battalions which were numbered, but whose numbers bore no relation to those of existing militia regiments. Two of the earliest overseas units raised in Montreal contained men drawn from such diverse regiments as the Black Watch, the Fusiliers de Mont-Royal, the Canadian Grenadier Guards, the Victoria Rifles, and a field battery. At a later time, some of the overseas battalions were broken up again to provide drafts and replacements. The original error, as it is now generally recognized to be, had unfortunate effects in Montreal. It took no account of the strong family attachment of Montrealers to certain established militia regiments. More damagingly, it took no account of the French-Canadian soldier's natural wish to be in a unit which spoke his language and to be commanded in his own language. Offers to raise entire French-Canadian battalions were refused. It was not till November 1914 that the recruiting of a French-Canadian unit, then known as the Twenty-Second Battalion, now as the Royal Twenty-Second Regiment, was authorized. Later, it is true, other French-Canadian formations were raised, but much of the initial ardour had been lost.

Montreal soldiers took part in every major engagement in which Canadians were involved. They were present at the Second Battle of Ypres, in April 1915, and at the storming of the Hindenburg Line in October 1918. On November 11, about an hour before the Armistice came into effect, Montreal troops entered Mons, from which the British had retreated in August 1914. Montrealers had fought the war to a full, victorious, conclusion. Finally, it was to Montreal that Canada's most distinguished soldier came. In April 1920, Sir Arthur Currie, the Commander of the Canadian Corps, was appointed Principal of McGill University.

The voluntary form of recruiting was continued till 1917. In Montreal it produced uneven results, but this was also true elsewhere. The two universities, Université de Montréal (as it soon was to become) and McGill both provided hospital and medical units, raised from their own staffs and students. Both universities had officer training corps, which prepared a steady stream of young men for the commissioned ranks of the army. Actually, they were to be found in all ranks, commissioned or not. They seem to have been attracted by extremes. Large numbers enlisted in heavy siege batteries; equally large numbers, in drafts for the Princess Patricia's Canadian Light Infantry.[8] By 1917, college-bred recruits were volunteering for service with the Royal Flying Corps, the Royal Canadian Air Force being as yet unknown. The large British immigrant population of Montreal also provided a substantial number of recruits.

Outside these groups, the volunteering method of recruiting yielded a decreasing number of men. The federal government gave high priority to employment in war industry and war farming. Thus the pool of manpower, never large, was further depleted. Writing at a later time, *La Presse* regretted that conscription for military service had not been adopted at the outbreak of war, when it would have been accepted readily. There was little to warrant this assumption, as *La Presse* should have learned when its windows were broken in the course of the anti-conscription riots of 1917. The Military Service Act, as the conscription measure was officially called, was adopted in the summer of 1917. It provoked disturbances in Montreal, culminating in anti-draft protests and in the attempted dynamiting (August 1917) of the house of Sir Hugh Graham, the proprietor of *The Montreal Star*. This journal had made itself conspicuous in its support of conscription. Early it had declared: "We ought to prepare to pour men like a flood into the fray . . . whether we can arm and equip them or not." It would have been strange if some Montrealers had not taken the *Star* at its word—especially those who were to be thrown against the enemy with no better weapons than their bare hands.

In the autumn of 1917, the federal general election produced a majority in favour of compulsory military service. It was secured virtually entirely outside Quebec. In Quebec, only three Unionists (that is to say, pro-conscription candidates) were returned—all from Montreal but all from English-speaking constituencies. The cry of one of the French-Canadian leaders rang true: "Conscription threatens to destroy . . . unity and to give rise throughout the country to deep internal divisions of long duration." If for "country" the term "city" is substituted, the foreboding was equally applicable to Montreal.

Ordinary city administration suffered distraction. The war greatly increased costs. Taxation, although high, failed to provide for more than basic services. Large-scale projects could not be financed and were laid aside. A substantial number of civic employees enlisted. The city, indeed, encouraged recruiting by promising job security and seniority rights to those who volunteered. These men were difficult to replace; so, there was an inevitable decline in administrative efficiency. Nevertheless, in its encouragement of national service and in other directions, the city had an enviable record. Appeals for patriotic and relief funds were officially supported; so, too, the sale of War, or Victory, bonds. Médéric Martin exercised his not inconsiderable diplomatic skill in smoothing over the disturbances occasioned by conscription.

Despite these strains, Montreal had a notable role in war production. Its machine shops were among the most advanced in Canada; its workers, among the most skilled. The Canadian and overseas governments alike were quick to take advantage of this expertise. As early as January 1915 the Angus shops of the Canadian Pacific began the manufacture of shells, having first designed and constructed the machinery that was required. The shops also undertook the instruction of munition workers. Some of them were trained from what must have seemed very unlikely material, men who had been thrown out of other employment in the first chaotic months of the war. Before the end of the war, women formed a large part of the work force.[9] The employment of women was not a novelty, although their employment in heavy industry was, in the experience of Montreal.

The most spectacular products of Montreal's war industry were the submarines. The shipyard had grown out of the Canadian armament program. In 1910, Parliament passed the Naval Service Act, which provided for, among other things, the building of war vessels. A Montreal group, of which Frederick Orr Lewis was the most active member, resolved to turn Montreal into a Canadian Toulon or Clydebank. Lewis was the agent for Vickers, Maxim, and Sons, the British armament makers. He persuaded Vickers to incorporate in Canada and to lay out its plant in Montreal. With the assistance of the Montreal Harbour Commission, an area east of the city was developed for the shipyard and its auxiliary engineering and electrical plants. In 1912, the floating dock *Duke of Connaught,* arrived from the United Kingdom. This plan to build Canadian warships was not implemented; so Montreal was deprived of being the birthplace of the Canadian navy. However, between 1915 and 1917, twenty-four submarines were built for the British, Italian, and Russian governments.[10] The shipyard increased Montreal's industrial potential. And, like the railway and electrical shops of an earlier time, it served as an advanced institution of technical education: a "practical school room in which young Canadians were taught."

War production was maintained in the face of increasing difficulties. Shortages in food and fuel made themselves unpleasantly felt by 1917. Wages failed to match the rapid rise of wartime living. By the end of the war, the unskilled workers in Montreal were earning about sixteen dollars a week, approximately two dollars less than the going rate elsewhere. It was against this grey background that the Armistice came in November 1918. Its reception in Montreal was tempered by the epidemic of Spanish influenza. There were said to be over sixteen thousand cases, of which nearly three thousand were fatal. Although not the last, the influenza was the most virulent of all early twentieth-century epidemics. Finally, the last weeks of the year found Montreal in the grip of a firemen's and policemen's strike. At issue were wages. When these were improved, the men, whose callings were the most dangerous in Montreal, willingly went back to duty.

The war ended on a note of tension. The anxieties and hardships of four years exacted their toll. The lowered vitality that made Montrealers easy victims of influenza had its counterpart in a lowered morale and lowered morality that rendered them complacent under mis-government for many years to come.

16 PROSPERITY DEPRESSION WAR

In the thirty years following the Armistice of 1918, Montreal passed through the successive experiences of prosperity, depression, and war. Between the three were strong connections, since prosperity bred depression and depression bred war.

PROSPERITY

The period opened with the currents of the war running strongly. When the Montreal troops came home from overseas, they were rapturously received. In 1919, the Prince of Wales, the future Edward VIII, made the first of those royal visits that were to become so familiar. The city took the Prince to itself. There were lavish entertainments in his honour. A review of troops was held, followed by the presentation of decorations. The saluting-point was on Sherbrooke Street, opposite the Art Gallery. In the words of the president of the Art Association: "I went . . . early . . . but it was almost impossible to cross Sherbrooke street. . . . The people [were]crowded on the steps, in the porch, under the pillars, and even on the window sills. . . . The prince had to come up all the steps. . . . We saw him struggling through the crowd, at times being lifted off his feet. Finally, he was shot into the front door, almost on his hands and knees, breathless and dishevelled, saying 'My God! I never saw such a crowd.' " Nor was the sequel unexpected. "The mayor [Martin] appeared, and offered to control the crowd so that the prince could reach the saluting-point, but his efforts were in vain. The crowd, who were largely English-speaking, hooted the mayor and jeered."[1]

Montreal shared in the general recovery that came to Canada following the First War. Its traditional position in transportation and finance was enhanced. In

1923, the head offices of the newly established Canadian National Railways were placed in Montreal. With one of the components of the Canadian National, the Grand Trunk, Montreal had had a very long and close connection; that with the Canadian Northern was more recent; with the Grand Trunk Pacific and the National Transcontinental, there had been no connection at all. The officers of the new railway, drawn from all parts of Canada, strengthened the economic and social fabric of Montreal. On the other hand, in their movement about the country on railway business, they represented Montreal to Canada. In this character, the city had few more acceptable ambassadors than Sir Henry Thornton, the first president of the Canadian National. Since Montreal was already the headquarters of the Canadian Pacific, it followed that the centre of control of Canada's two major railways was located in Montreal.

The improvement of Montreal's financial position was less obvious—although not less important. During the first quarter of the century, three new banks were organized, the Banque Provinciale (1900), the Royal Bank of Canada (1910), and the Banque Canadienne Nationale (1925).[2] Montreal's banks had not been concerned very closely with the construction of the later railways. Accordingly, they were not affected by the railways' near-bankruptcy, the cause of the government's taking possession of them and of their amalgamation in the Canadian National system. The position of all the Montreal banks was more positively strengthened by the rise of the newsprint industry in Quebec and by the expansion of hydroelectric plants. Developments along these lines compensated Montreal for the relatively small part it had had in the mining boom of the period. The rewards in that field had gone chiefly to Toronto. Yet Montreal managed to derive benefit from Toronto's prosperity. Montreal interests secured control of what was described as "Toronto's largest and most influencial newspaper."[3] It was a Montreal corporation that built and owned Toronto's largest and most palatial hotel, the Royal York.

The most conspicuous evidence of Montreal's enjoyment of prosperity was the transformation of the city's skyline. In 1913 and 1914, the great tower was added to the Windsor Station and the cornerstone of the Sun Life Building laid. In 1933, the final stages of the central block of the latter were completed. The dates 1913-33 not inaccurately cover the period. Other notable buildings were the Bell Telephone on Beaver Hall Hill and the Royal Bank on St. James Street. In 1928, construction was begun on the new home for the Université de Montréal on the northern slopes of Mount Royal. All of these carried forward established preference for Romanesque, Classical, or French Renaissance design.

Unfortunately, not all this new development was gain. Too often, the fine buildings grew out of slums or reared themselves in the sight of slums. A host of social agencies, Red Feather, Catholic Charities, Jewish Philanthropies, and others were called into being to alleviate distress. In the universities, departments of sociology were set up to wrestle with the paradox of poverty in the midst of affluence.

In another direction, there was little sign of advance. The alliance of business and municipal and provincial politics was firm. The retirement of Sir Lomer Gouin as the premier of Quebec in 1920 removed the only genuinely progressive force. It also removed a premier who lacked sympathy with Martin's type. Gouin's successor in the premiership, Alexandre Taschereau, had nothing of Gouin's zeal for good causes. Certainly, he had no feeling for Montreal; no real connection with the city.

In 1921, Martin led the attack on the progressives' effort to impose commission government on Montreal. The Quebec provincial administration had lent a somewhat wavering support, and the new instrument was to be made acceptable by means of a referendum. In this instance, the weapon was turned against its friends, for Martin secured the defeat of the plan by the very referendum that was to have brought it in. Since the commission form of government had had the blessing of the province, Martin advertised its defeat as a victory for civic autonomy. Shortly afterwards, Médéric Martin was made a legislative councillor, a member of the Quebec upper house. The honour was regarded generally as an act of appeasement on the part of the provincial cabinet.

The accommodation between provincial and municipal governments sometimes seemed very one-sided. In 1919, Montreal was induced to annex Maisonneuve, to stave off the latter's insolvency. In 1925, the Protestant school boards of Montreal and the surrounding towns were amalgamated to strengthen the financial position of one of them, Verdun. The plight of the Verdun Protestant schools was not brought about by extravagance or mismanagement. It was occasioned by the fact that Roman Catholic owners of apartments or tenements paid no taxes to Protestant schools, even when the children of their tenants attended them. Since the rights of private property were sacrosanct, the provincial legislature refused to consider a division of the property tax in Verdun; rather, it made the difficulties of the Verdun Protestants the responsibility of Montreal Protestants in general. The long-term results of the school adjustment were significant: the Protestant School Board of Greater Montreal, as the general supervisory body finally became known, was the earliest effective governing and administrating unit in the metropolitan area.

The success of school amalgamation was in contrast to the unfruitful attempt to secure political co-operation. In 1921, the province set up the Montreal Metropolitan Commission (11 George V, cap. 140). The short-range objective of this body was to supervise the finances of certain towns on the Island of Montreal. At longer range, it was hoped that the Commission would co-ordinate development over the entire metropolitan area. In 1921, this was very forward-looking indeed. However, it is only fair to state that the way had been pointed, twelve years before, by G. - A. Nantel's *La métropole de demain.* This pioneer political study of urbanism was a counterpart of Ames's earlier sociological one, *The City Below the Hill.* Nantel had advocated federation as the best means of rationalizing Montreal's and the suburbs' growth. The costliness of the annexations between 1909 and 1918 must have lent weight to Nantel's theories. Unfortunately, the Metropolitan Commission was a very imperfect instrument. Its operations left none of the customers satisfied, Montreal or the suburbs.

In the sustained glow of business and political one-ness, the Tramways Company and the Montreal Light, Heat and Power Consolidated continued to prosper. The latter consolidated its position in fact as well as in name. It came to terms with potential rivals, Shawinigan and Beauharnois, and systematically snuffed out small, publicly owned electric companies. Between 1928 and 1933, every municipal system on the Island of Montreal, with the exception of that of Westmount, was eliminated. Such were the victories of free enterprise in a favourable political climate.

Of more general benefit were the improvements made in the port of Montreal. By the 1920's, it had taken on much of its modern appearance. Deep-water basins, grain elevators, transit sheds, and an extensive electric railway pointed to the port's function—the expedition of the outward movement of cereals and the inward movement of foreign-manufactured goods. Equally indicative of its function were the provisions made for immigrants. As early as World War I, there had been evidences of new developments. The first stage centred on the Vickers property with its shipyards and dry dock. Then followed the extension of the harbour works eastward, the part particularly associated with the 1920's. This area provided natural deep-water berthing for vessels and was well adapted for the handling of such specialized freights as coal and petroleum. The rise in demand for these commodities was a finger-post pointing to the new character of Montreal as an industrial city.

The last years of the 1920's were taken up with the construction of a second bridge across the St. Lawrence at Montreal. More than two decades before, the old Victoria Bridge, designed for railway service, had been completely rebuilt. The iron tube had given way to the familiar steel-truss construction, and a roadway had been added. The rebuilt bridge was known patriotically as the Victoria Jubilee. On July 14, 1899, a horse and buggy had made the first crossing, a modest anticipation of the highway traffic of later times. The second bridge was designed for road use exclusively. (The provision of a tram-line, although contemplated, was not carried out.) On May 24, 1930, the Jacques-

Cartier Bridge, as it was appropriately called, was formally dedicated by the Anglican Bishop and the Roman Catholic Auxiliary Archbishop of Montreal.

The harbour of Montreal was Canada's doorway to the outer world. It attracted shipping not only from Europe but from South Africa, South America, Australia, and New Zealand.[4] In it the house flags of the major shipping firms were seen; the scarlet and white checker-board of the Canadian Pacific from 1903; the blue of the Cunard from 1911. In 1916, however, the oldest of them all, the tricolour of the Allan ships, disappeared when that line was absorbed by the Canadian Pacific. The port was thronged by seamen of all nations. They were marked by their rolling gait; their strange speech; and the outlandish wares they tried to vend—parrots, monkeys, and scrimshaw. Two services were provided for them. As far back as 1862, the Montreal Sailors' Institute (originally undertaken by the YMCA) had been founded; more recently, in 1893, the Catholic Sailors' Club. These institutions provided religious and social facilities, the latter being changed to meet the preferences of the younger seamen of the war and post-war years. In 1919, as one of the events in his crowded Montreal visit, the Prince of Wales laid the cornerstone of the Sailors' Memorial Tower on the end of the Victoria Pier. It was also a monument to Montreal's dependence on its port.

Two developments in the harbour were to be of continuing importance. After its wartime construction of ships, Vickers began the building of aircraft.[5] They included the Viking, an amphibian that was to be widely used in northern surveying and prospecting. Here was a clear foreshadowing of Montreal's place in aviation. Secondly, the harbour attracted an industry closely associated with aviation. In the last days of 1916, the Imperial Oil Company's refinery at Montreal East went into production. With the distribution of petroleum products, initially kerosene, Montreal had had experience reaching back to the 1880's. Refining was entirely new. Along with the refinery and storage plant, a dock was built, for the river as a means of bringing in the crude petroleum had been a major factor in the selection of the site. (At a later time, during the Second

World War, a pipe line would be built to Portland, in order to supplement the supply brought in by ship.) The refining plants of other oil companies followed; McColl-Frontenac (modern Texaco) and British-American, both before 1930. It was a demonstration of Montreal's happy geographical position that petroleum refining and distributing for much of eastern Canada would be centred in its port.[6]

THE
ST. LAWRENCE
SEAWAY
THE FIRST PHASE

In harbour development, Montreal led and Canada was the beneficiary. In the instance of the St. Lawrence Seaway, or Deep Waterway as it was usually called in the 1920's, Montreal was certainly not the leader; nor, was it argued, would Montreal be a beneficiary.[7] The strength of Montreal's opposition in the first phase of the Seaway project is an index of the vigour of traditional interests as late as the second decade of the twentieth century.

By the 1920's, the project had taken on recognizable outlines; the St. Lawrence was to be deepened between Montreal and Cornwall to provide electricity and to permit the movement of large vessels. Both aspects were highly disturbing: electrical production might jeopardize the monopoly enjoyed by the power combine, improved navigation might threaten the numerous interests that depended upon the character of the city as the junction of ocean and inland travel. The Montreal press, never more the apoligist of the ruling class, entered a noisy protest. The Quebec government was wheeled into line. It advanced an adroit defence; provincial control over natural resources. Nevertheless, there was dissent. Manufacturers who used electricity were becoming increasingly restive under the rates levied by the power combine.

At the end of the 1920's, an elaborate compromise was worked out. In 1929, the Beauharnois Power Corporation was chartered. It was discreetly "neutral" (in its president's phrase) regarding navigational improvements. However, it undertook to respect navigation rights and to surrender its canal to the federal government on demand. Sale of electricity was to be made through the Montreal Light, Heat and Power Consolidated, which in this way retained its monopoly. Unfortunately, Beauharnois became synonymous with scandal rather than with either electrical production or navigation.

This confused and apparently inconclusive episode has a place in Montreal's history. In the local sense, the division of opinion regarding electrical production showed the restiveness of new interests under the old economic leadership. The new interests, chiefly manufacturing, were not able to assert themselves; certainly, they were not able to break the hold of the old order over the press. In the larger sense, that of metropolitan ascendancy, Montreal's refusal shows the long survival of the concept of the city as a transit-centre or point of transhipment. The opening of deep water navigation above Montreal seemed bound to reduce the queen of river cities to just another river town.

THE
SIXTIETH ANNIVERSARY
OF CONFEDERATION

The celebrations in 1927 of the sixtieth anniversary of Confederation provided an appropriate climax for the prosperous period of the 1920's. Montreal's celebrations were sited, with becoming historical sense, at the foot of the commanding statue of Sir George-Etienne Cartier that stands on Fletcher's Fields. (Not that the other founding fathers were forgotten. The graves of McGee and Galt in Côte des Neiges and Mount Royal cemeteries were piled high with flowers.) On the hot July first morning Montrealers gathered to hear the reading of the message of the governor general and the resolutions of the city council. The governor general spoke from Ottawa. The still novel radio brought his words to the ears of Montrealers by means of loudspeakers set up in the Park. This must rank as the earliest public use of the medium in Montreal, and probably as the first national use on this continent— over a year before the employment of radio in the United States presidential campaign of 1928.

In the afternoon, there was a great turnout of school cadets, Boy Scouts, and Girl Guides at Parc La Fontaine. In the evening, the eastern slopes of Mount Royal were again crowded, as the Société Saint-Jean-Baptiste held a monster rally. It was addressed by Henri Bourassa and by Mgr Olivier Maurault, who was then the *curé* of Notre Dame. In moving phrases, Bourassa warned his fellow countrymen against self-imposed isolation within Canada. Mgr Maurault spoke on the subject of national unity. He concluded his address by a quotation from Cartier's "O Canada! mon pays, mes amours!" Cartier had composed and sung the hymn over ninety years before at the first meeting of the Société Saint-Jean-Baptiste. It was taken up and rendered again with immense verve as a fitting climax to the celebrations of the sixtieth year of Confederation.

Inevitably, comparison is invited between the First Dominion Day and the sixtieth. The sixtieth was very much a Canadian occasion. The troops and sailors massed about the Cartier monument were Canadian. The mayor who presided was a French Canadian. The flag so proudly displayed was the Canadian ensign. Montreal had come a long way in national consciousness. It was destined to go an even longer way between the sixtieth Dominion Day and the one hundredth.

Comparison is invited also between the austerity of Confederation and the relative luxury of sixty years later. By 1927, many things that add comfort to present-day living were in general use: the synthetic fibre rayon, electric refrigerators, oil furnaces, and radios. The automobile had taken on much of its modern reliability and some of its refinements, such as a hard top, four-wheel brakes, and low-pressure tires (the tubeless ones came later). Road surfacing with asphalt, a by-product of the petroleum refining, made motoring safer and more comfortable. In the late summer of 1928, Montreal had its first moving-picture theatre designed specifically for sound. The year before, action and sound had been synchronized in *The Jazz Singer* and the talkie age had begun. Even television was on the way—though it took another twenty years or so to come into general use. On September 1, 1928, the Montreal press reported the television displays of the fifth radio exposition, held in Berlin.

The sixtieth year was notable also for the advance made in air service. In September 1927, the first airmail flights began between Montreal and Rimouski on the lower St. Lawrence, where transatlantic steamers were met. In the same autumn an even more promising move was made, when the British government selected Montreal as the western terminal of its airship service. Great hopes were pinned on airships or dirigibles. It was believed that they could make long flights on regularly designated routes, much as liners did on the ocean. Between 1927 and 1930, a base was laid out at St. Hubert, about ten miles south of Montreal. Its most conspicuous feature was the mooring mast for the dirigibles. The mast was used only once, in the summer of 1930, when the R-100 made an experimental voyage.[8] It was entirely successful, but disaster to a sister ship and the heavy cost of operation caused the project to be cancelled. Nevertheless, Montreal's claims were recognized: in July 1937, the first flight by a heavier-than-air machine from Britain reached Montreal; and two years later to the month, the same aircraft, the *Caledonia*, a flying boat of the Imperial Airways, returned to inaugurate regular mail-carrying service. By a striking coincidence, in July 1937, the first regular transcontinental mail flight was made from Montreal. It was by the Trans-Canada Air Lines, later known as Air Canada.

THE END
OF THE
MARTIN ERA

In 1928, Martin's administration had the outward appearance of strength. Only two years before, he had disposed of two opponents, winning with a majority of twenty-nine thousand over the closer. In fact, Martin had won every mayoralty election but one since 1914. In 1924, he had been defeated by Charles Duquette, a spokesman for the rising French-Canadian middle class. Perhaps if he had been younger and the 1920's more inclined to political experiment, Duquette might have anticipated the triumphs of Jean Drapeau. However, he was content with a single term.

The appearance of strength was deceptive. In the spring of 1927, Martin's position was shaken by two misfortunes. In January, over seventy children were killed, crushed to death rather than burned, in a moving-picture theatre fire—the Laurier Palace disaster. In March and April, Montreal was gripped by a typhoid fever epidemic. Some three thousand persons became sick, of whom about two hundred died. Both tragedies pointed directly to laxity in administration. In the instance of the theatre, the city had not enforced its own safety measures. In the panic following the cry of "Fire," the children were trampled to death, because the exit doors had not worked properly. In the instance of the typhoid, the dereliction was even more glaring. A milk-pasteurization by-law had been imposed on an apathetic city council, but it was not enforced. In the face of protests by private organizations, and even by its own health office, the council did nothing to ascertain the cause of the typhoid outbreak, nor even to provide emergency treatment. Vaccination clinics were set up in the Sun Life Building on Dominion Square and elsewhere, maintained and staffed by private endeavour. Finally, the provincial government acted, and, on its authority, closed two dairies alleged to be the source of the contaminated milk. Throughout the crisis, the Mayor displayed conspicuous lack of interest, to say nothing of vigour. It is a commentary on the new civic sense that this would be held against him a year later when the municipal elections were due.

As they approached in April 1928, a further episode discredited Médéric Martin. It was discovered that he had lent his name to brewery promotion. La Brasserie Mont-Royal undertook to pay him a royalty (six cents on three dozen bottles) in return for his recommending the company's stock and product, *la bière Martin.* The failure of the company brought the adventure into the open. The pettiness of it made Martin an object of ridicule. Possibly he would have survived, had not his principal opponent been Camillien Houde, the most accomplished actor in Montreal's political history.

WHO'S HOUDE?

Who's Houde? The question was not entirely rhetorical, for Camillien Houde was a little-known man when he entered the mayoralty contest of 1928. The time would come when he would be called "Monsieur Montréal," the very embodiment of the city over which he presided.[9] In 1928, however, he seemed to be a David pitted against the Goliath Médéric Martin. In that contest two generations met. The victory was with youth and Houde (he was only thirty-nine). In office or out, Houde was a compelling figure in Montreal for nearly thirty years.

The election followed easily predictable lines. Houde poked fun at the poor man who had become wealthy in the service of his fellow citizens. Martin was exhibited as the *seigneur* of Laval-des-Rapides, the Mayor's country home, where he hob-nobbed with the great and forgot the humble people on whose backs he had climbed to affluence. Martin's foibles were ruthlessly exposed: the celebrated "toga," the confection of mink and ermine that he had added to the mayor's official costume; the brilliantly polished *crachoir,* which occupied such a conspicuous place in the council chamber beside the mayor's seat. No doubt any form of personal rule is vulnerable to ridicule, and Martin's twelve years at the city hall provided ample opportunity for the artist. For the first time, he was put on the defensive.

For the first time too, Martin was confronted by an opponent whose origins were quite as popular as his own. Houde was a poor man's son. He had known real poverty. His preliminary education had been at the hands of the Christian Brothers, traditionally the teach-ers of the poor. In breadth of field, Houde could easily outclass Martin, whose appeal had been to the skilled, or semi-skilled workingman, who was, nevertheless, a property owner. Houde's was much wider. It was to the new city proletariat: the retail clerks; the bus drivers; delivery men; the casually employed. Camillien Houde had no skilled trade; no profession. He had worked behind the counter in a shop. He had become a bank clerk, and later a bank inspector. Thus he spoke for the new masses; the employees of the great corpora-tions; the anonymous, whose lives were filled with uncertainty. Houde spoke also for a new generation. He communicated directly with his contemporaries. They gave him a majority of nearly twenty-two thousand (21,799).[10]

Camillien Houde was hailed immediately as an inspired amateur. This was far from the truth, although when it suited his purpose Houde used the phrase himself. He had been a member of the Quebec Legis-lative Assembly since 1923, when he had stood as a Conservative. In the dreary years after the conscription controversy of the First World War, this required cour-age. Throughout his provincial campaigns, Houde enjoyed the goodwill of organized labour. He enjoyed something more than that from William Tremblay, the federal Member for Maisonneuve. The reality is that Houde was a skilled and tough practitioner, who adroitly balanced municipal and provincial politics to his advantage. In 1929, Houde became the leader of the Conservative opposition in the Quebec legislature, just the year following his spectacular triumph in the Montreal mayoralty. There is no reasonable doubt that his provincial position was effectively used to score another municipal victory, in 1930, when he won the mayoralty again.

To that point, Houde's riding of two horses had been remarkably successful. He was, however, unable or unwilling to bestride three. At the time of the federal elections in the summer of 1930, he was strangely inactive, although he had an open invitation to go on from his municipal and provincial position of strength. His failure to do so was most unfortunate, for the Conservatives won and did not forget. The next year, 1931, they stood aside and allowed the blow to fall on Houde at the time of the provincial elections. His party was defeated, and he himself lost in the two constituencies he contested. A year later, (1932) the Conservatives were still unappeased. Houde received no support in the Montreal municipal elections, when he was resoundingly beaten by Fernand Rinfret.

Nor was this the nadir. The Quebec provincial Conservatives had become disillusioned with Houde, and in 1932 they held a party caucus at which he was displaced. The choice of successor fell on Maurice Duplessis, whose path, from this point, was constantly to cross that of Houde.[11] The two men were unsympathetic at the start and grew mutually embittered. In 1934, Houde became Mayor of Montreal for the third time, and in 1936, Duplessis, for the first time, became Premier of Quebec. Montreal lost too: in the later 1920's, Houde was making some progress towards reconciling municipal and provincial points of view, a subject of increasing importance in modern Montreal history; his replacement by Duplessis divided city and province again and added the bitterness of personal animosity.

DEPRESSION
THE 1930's

Within two years after the diamond jubilee of Confederation, Montreal experienced the onset of depression. In the last weeks of October 1929, panic-selling gripped the Montreal Stock Exchange. It closed with stocks registering heavy losses. Four days later, there was a second panic. These local events coincided with the collapse of stock markets in New York and elsewhere. The market failures, dramatic and certainly disastrous, were, however, more the signs than the causes of the depression that followed. This was emphatically so in Montreal. The great monopolies had been remarkably insensitive. They had poured money into gigantic office buildings—monuments to extravagance. There was little corresponding advance in plant construction or in productive capacity. Nor was there any significant rise in wages. In addition to these weaknesses, there was another: Montreal's reliance on its traditional role as the place of transhipment of goods. Although that role was passing, it still dominated the city's economic thinking. Montreal was vulnerable to disasters that happened far away, either in its Canadian hinterland or in its European market. The coincidence of disaster in those two areas, along with the unco-ordinated and top-heavy growth of business, accounts for the severity and duration of the depression.

Large-scale unemployment became the most agonizing of Montreal's many problems. By 1934, when Houde returned to the mayoralty, about one quarter of the city's population of over 900,000 was receiving public assistance of one kind or another. The city's finances, partly because of the heavy relief payments, were in a most perilous state. Houde's contributions to mitigating the crisis were entirely personal. He was essentially conservative, and reacted instinctively away from revolutionary, or even radical, solutions. Early and late he was in his office, ready to listen and sympathize, and, where he could, to aid. The unfortunates were left in no doubt as to his solicitude, and, since he was confronted by personal problems, perhaps his personal approach was the best. Greater collaboration with Quebec might have been helpful, but ten days after the Duplessis administration was formed in August 1936, Houde resigned. In the politicians' eyes, he had served his purpose: Mackenzie King, the Prime Minister, remarked: "S'il n'y a pas eu d'émeute à Montréal, c'est à vous, monsieur Houde, que nous le devons." [12]

The depression spread over nearly ten years and entered into every phase of Montreal life. Unemployment became endemic. Little new construction was undertaken; existing houses went unrepaired. Over a thousand houses officially designated as being unfit for human habitation were, nevertheless, inhabited— because there were no others. Private philanthropic agencies, along with the city's welfare department and the provincial and federal governments, sought to mitigate the worst effects of unemployment. Nevertheless, though actual starvation was warded off, nothing could be done to relieve the monotony of workless days; the anxiety as savings ebbed; the wearing thin of morale.

The wearing thin was not slow. At the beginning, there was the stimulus of combat; a sense of comradeship in privation. There was also the strong tradition of charity, especially in Montreal's French and Irish past. The Anglican Bishop, John Cragg Farthing, commented on the generous support his appeals had received. They were made in the autumn of 1930, on behalf of young harvesters, who, unable to find jobs in prairie wheatlands, returned destitute to Montreal.[13] A year later, harshness manifested itself. The press gave lurid and melodramatic accounts of collisions between police and unemployed. What were described as "international 'red' demonstrations" were systematically broken up: "No truncheons were used . . . but they [a breadline] were hustled by the free use of fists." The Recorder was applauded for his firmness. He sentenced an unemployed man brought before him to three months hard labour, on the grounds that he had remained in Montreal (at the Meurling Refuge) when he knew that there was no work in the city. This person had compounded crime by obstruction. On being apprehended, he had plucked the constable by the arm, saying that he was arresting the wrong man. As he was led away, the man had raised the seditious cry: "Come on comrades! Down with the police!" or "Allons mes camarades! A bas les pieds plats!"— according to whether one read an English or a French newspaper.

There was present in Montreal the outlook that had bred national socialism in Europe. Indeed, there was a small National Social Christian party, complete with swastika flags, salutes, and shirts. Christian in this context simply meant anti-Jewish. Old-standing cultural or charitable organizations of Montrealers of German or Italian ancestry were made the objects of vigorous propaganda drives by the respective consuls. The visit of the German training-cruiser *Nuremberg* in 1937 was the occasion of very highly organized (and publicized) demonstrations. Proportionately, it attracted more attention than the visit the following summer of HMS *Ajax*. (Both vessels saw service in the early years of the Second Great War: *Nuremberg* was severely damaged in the naval operations off Norway. *Ajax* achieved fame in the destruction of the pocket-battleship *Graf Spee*.)

Dissatisfaction with the existing order began to be expressed by native Montrealers too. There was *nostalgie de pouvoir fort* and yearning for *ordre moral*. Criticism was not restricted to Montreal. The Premier of Quebec wondered "[Whether] democracy had not gone too far? Whether Mussolini was not sometimes right?" The *Star* was less guarded: "The great advantages the Fascist nations have over [the] democratic is not their unquestionable superiority in effective organization . . . but . . . that they are governed by their best minds." In the autumn of 1935 Sir Edward Beatty, the president of the Canadian Pacific, even indulged in an attack on freedom of inquiry in higher education. It was a strange indictment for a man who was the chancellor of one university (McGill) to make at the convocation of another (the University of Western Ontario.)[14]

The position of Montreal's two universities was seriously affected by the hard times. The Université de Montréal was not able to occupy its new buildings on Mount Royal. Financial stringency forced it to carry on till the mid-1940's in the old crowded quarters on St. Denis Street. There, its great teachers, such as Brother Marie-Victorin of the Institut Botanique, taught and wrote in make-shift laboratories and basement class rooms. McGill had financial problems as well. Its revenues (which at that time came chiefly from investments) were so depleted that, to make both ends meet, salaries were drastically cut and fees were increased by fifty per cent. Tactics of this kind scarcely reflected credit on the Board of Governors recruited from the financial élite of Montreal. Following the death of Sir Arthur Currie in 1933, McGill experienced two brief principalships (those of Eustace Morgan and Lewis Douglas, 1935-40), with inevitable loss in continuity. Indirectly, the university also suffered from a controversy that had arisen in one of the affiliated theological colleges. The conservative governors effectively got rid of an instructor whose advanced social views they deplored, by abolishing the academic chair he held.

A drastic answer to Montreal's numerous difficulties was supplied by the province in 1940. It placed the city temporarily under the tutelage of the Municipal Commission, a new agency set up to administer financially embarrassed municipalities. At the same time, it devised a new form of city government—the twelfth since 1833, when Montreal got its first charter.[15] The membership of the council was increased to ninety-nine. A third of this number was chosen by the property owners—Category A; a third, by all the citizens—Category B; a third, by various public bodies such as the Chambre de Commerce, the Board of Trade, and the universities—Category C. The council chose a six-man executive committee from its members, and the committee in turn chose a chairman. In addition to this imposing legislative and executive body was a mayor, elected by all the people. The new charter certainly made Montreal safe for the propertied. They chose a full third of the council in their own right and they had a voice in the election of the other two thirds. The property owners formed far fewer than a third of the population—or for that matter of the enfranchised. Very great authority lay with the chairman of the executive committee. Nevertheless, the mayor presided at the meeting of the council, and, in other public gatherings, took precedence.

PRELUDE TO WAR

On the events leading to World War II, Montreal was well informed. The reporting of foreign news by its press was among the best in Canada. By way of contrast, editorial comment on it was slight, and news coverage of local events was very poor. *The Gazette* so completely buried in its back pages the typhoid epidemic of 1927 that all but its most patient readers might have supposed that Montreal was enjoying the rosiest of good health. *La Presse* loaded its columns with obituary pictures and notices. However consoling they may have been to the bereaved, they were a poor substitute for critical local news. In the early summer of 1940, the *Star* lavished on Winston Churchill the same praise that it had, until recently, lavished on Neville Chamberlain, the excoriation of whom was Churchill's stock-in-trade. The *Star* itself experienced a change of ownership. In 1933, the newspaper was sold by Lord Atholstan to J. H. McConnell. The transfer, however, did not become effective until after Atholstan's death in 1938. Nor did the transfer produce any very discernible change in policy, since Mr. McConnell, like Lord Atholstan, was interested in advertising revenue. A corrective to the inadequacies of the newspapers was provided by the radio. In 1936, the Canadian Broadcasting Corporation was established. Its programs, as well as those of independently owned stations, frequently broke the conspiracy of silence enjoined by the press.

The exception made for the Spanish Civil War was striking. From its beginning in 1936 until its end in 1939, it roused interest and controversy—although almost entirely one-sided. The sympathies of the Montreal possessing classes, irrespective of race, were arrayed with the Spanish Nationalists and Generalisimo Franco. The Caudillo's orthodoxy, his firmness towards labour, and his soundness on communism excused the awkward fact that he was the leader of a rebellion.

In October 1936, the city found itself in the hands of Montreal university students, who paraded the streets shouting, "A bas les communistes: à bas les apostolats." The outburst was prompted by the arrival of four spokesmen to plead the cause of the legitimate government of Spain. Two of them were women, one a priest (a Franciscan, the Reverend Luis Sarasola), and one a former Minister of Education. The civil authorities allowed themselves to be browbeaten into forbidding the Spaniards to speak publicly. The chairman of the executive committee assured the students: "We will not allow Communism to take root here." This despite the fact that the government of the Spanish Republic was not communist, nor was any one of the delegates. No protest was made against this flagrant surrender of the right of free speech except by a few bold spirits. Principal Morgan of McGill University entered a vigorous defence of his students who had made their Union available to the Spaniards. It was the choicest of ironies that on the eve of the centenary of the Rebellion of 1837, Montreal supported the very conditions that the *Patriotes* had died to end.[16]

In the spring of 1938, one of the Spanish fascist leaders was tendered a public reception. It was with some difficulty that the mayor, Adhémar Raynault, and the Roman Catholic Auxiliary Archbishop were prevailed on not to attend. Doubtless Montreal followed the line taken by the provincial administration. In 1937, the Duplessis government had passed the notorious Act Respecting Communist Propaganda—the padlock law. This measure was accepted without protest either by Montreal members of the provincial parliament or by the Montreal press. What support Montreal gave the democratic side in Spain was surreptitious. The recruiting of the Mackenzie-Papineau Battalion of the International Brigade was unheralded; its exploits, unsung.

To the other events of the appeasement era, a tired indifference was shown. Even the sufferings of German and Austrian Jews stirred little general interest. Local anti-Semitism, of which there was a good deal, took a particularly cowardly form. Jewish membership in certain clubs and fraternal societies was discouraged, or was subjected to a quota. It was widely believed that the same device was employed by schools. Jewish shopkeepers stood in peril of having their windows broken. During an expression of patriotic fervour, such as the mobbing of the Spanish Republican visitors, the police were accustomed to guard the newspaper offices of *The Jewish Eagle*. The final extinction of Czechoslovak liberties in the spring of 1939 received no more enduring memorial than a few slogans scribbled in chalk on the pavement of Victoria Square. The visit of King George VI and Queen Elizabeth in the early summer of 1939 certainly evoked a warm response. It was the first occasion on which a reigning monarch had visited Montreal. Yet the significance was lost in the attention lavished on patriotic details, parades, decorations, and so on. In September, war was declared. The fact that Canada made its declaration independently as a free nation went largely unnoted.

THE SECOND
WORLD WAR

For the first nine months, the war dragged. An attitude almost of cynicism was common in the quiet phase, September 1939 to June 1940. Montreal's response was not peculiar. Even the sinking of the *Athenia,* on which Montreal lives were lost, and the overrunning of Poland, a bitter blow to Montreal's large Polish community, roused none of the feeling that the sinking of the *Lusitania* or the invasion of Belgium had done twenty-odd years before. In spite of this tepid attitude, recruiting went forward. It was greatly strengthened by the employment of the historic militia units. In October, what was to become the new temper showed itself. Maurice Duplessis, the provincial premier, held an election in protest against the centralizing of economic and political power at Ottawa—something inescapable in time of war. The Duplessis line was immediately denounced as "an act of national sabotage." In the ensuing election he was decisively beaten. Montreal contributed to the overthrow, since it returned an almost solid Liberal bloc—eleven of its twelve members—to Quebec. (The twelfth was Camillien Houde, who stood as an independent.) At the end of the year, the First Canadian Division went overseas. It contained Montreal troops, who this time carried the familiar designations they had borne as militia regiments.

The events of 1940 swept away whatever remained of indifference. A sense of immediacy replaced the hesitancy of 1939. This was the spirit that sustained Montreal throughout the succeeding five years of war.

171

Its people accepted the restrictions (with some grumbling) that the Second World War demanded. In the summer of 1940, they registered under the National Resources Mobilization Act—in spite of Camillien Houde's advice that they should not. Houde, who had voluntarily retired in 1936, had returned to the municipal scene in 1938 and been elected mayor for the fourth time. In consequence of his advice, he was retired—involuntarily—to an internment camp until 1944.

Montreal became the centre of war production and of war distribution. Sometimes the two functions were combined. Aircraft, manufactured in Montreal or elsewhere in America, were flown to Europe from Dorval, where the Ferry Command maintained its headquarters. This was a striking indication, in modern circumstances, of the value of Montreal's earliest asset, its geographical position. Montreal made a great range of weapons and ammunition. It also built ships, both for the navy and for the merchant service. Many of the latter were constructed from prefabricated sections, the final assembly being made at Montreal. Montreal laboratories engaged in chemical research, particularly in explosives.

The city responded to the enlightened man-power policies of World War II. As has been pointed out, the First Canadian Division of 1939 was made up of the historic militia regiments. Although the army establishment was greatly increased, units with traditional titles, or with recognizable territorial titles, continued to be employed. In spite, therefore, of the changes imposed by twentieth-century warfare, in which hussars became reconnaissance troops, and guards, armoured corps, the invaluable continuity was maintained. The navy and airforce had different traditions from those of the army. There were no Montreal-manned ships or squadrons. Nevertheless, with both services, the city was closely identified. Recruiting and training were carried on in Montreal. The airforce brought to Montreal men from all over the Commonwealth and from some of the countries of occupied Europe, notably Poland, Norway, and France. A map of the theatres of operation would show that Montrealers, whether airmen, seamen, or soldiers, served in almost every one of them. Montreal women served also, since the Second World War provided them with the women's divisions of the armed forces. Recollection will always play round the exploits of Montreal troops in France and Italy. Two Montreal units, the Fusiliers de Mont-Royal and the Black Watch, took a conspicuous part in the raid on Dieppe, midsummer 1942. It was the return of many Montrealers to what may very well have been the port of departure of their ancestors three hundred years before.

17 THE GREAT TRANSFORMATION

After World War II, Montreal experienced transformation in virtually every department of its life. Some of the changes could be easily seen; others were less obvious. Some began before 1945. All, however, made themselves felt in the twenty-two years between V-J Day and the Centenary of Confederation.

Even Montreal's role in Canadian life was transformed. While this was largely the result of change within the city, it owed something to developments in other parts of Canada. The opening of the Panama Canal in 1914, the beginning of Arctic navigation in 1931, the improvement of the Halifax and Saint John harbours for commercial and passenger service, and, finally, the Seaway made Vancouver, Churchill, Halifax, Saint John, and Toronto all rivals in what had been Montreal's exclusive field. That Montreal did not sink into insignificance was due to its internal transformation.

THE NEW INDUSTRIALISM

The transformation of Montreal was made possible by two factors: prosperity and people. The city shared in the good times general in North America after the Second World War. The war had increased Montreal's industrial potential. The growing industry and population stimulated local developments, new housing, and so on. The diversity and increasing size of Montreal made it an important market in itself. Studies undertaken in the 1930's assailed the accepted view of Montreal as a transhipment point only.[1] The port handled a large volume of goods intended for local use. However, much of the general Canadian trade remained, and Montreal benefited from the good times enjoyed by the country as a whole.

Two new forces came into play. The earlier was the

exploitation of iron ore in northeastern Quebec; the later, the revival of the Seaway project. In 1947, the Iron Ore Company of Canada was formed to bring the field into production. (The ore had been discovered first in 1938.)[2] Montreal immediately felt the impulse. It was only about seven hundred miles by air from Knob Lake (Schefferville), the original centre of operations. Montreal became the point from which supplies were first flown in. With the opening of a railhead at Sept-Iles, heavy equipment was sent by boat from Montreal. Since the bulk of the ore was destined for inland mills in the United States, the most direct route was by way of the St. Lawrence. The insufficiency of the existing canal system was patent. A new argument was supplied for reviving the project of the St. Lawrence Deep Waterway.

The revival of the Seaway project (to use the modern name) was the second major factor in the economic transformation of Montreal. The Seaway was completed between 1954 and 1959. In terms of actual construction, only a relatively small section—St. Lambert-Caughnawaga—lay in the Montreal metropolitan area. (The Beauharnois canal, completed for power purposes in 1932, was adapted for shipping in 1956.) When one recalls the violence of the opposition at an earlier date, the equanimity with which the revived project was received was truly remarkable. The generation of the 1920's had passed away, or had prudently channelled its wealth into activities still reserved for private enterprise. The Montreal press passed from fatuous criticism to equally fatuous praise. The Seaway was formally opened in June 1959 by Queen Elizabeth. The ceremony took place at the St. Lambert Lock, the eastern entrance to the Seaway. It was probably not too far distant from the spot where Jacques Cartier had obtained his first sight of Montreal, over four hundred years before.

The Seaway extended along Montreal's latest frontier of development. This was the region variously called "the golden triangle" or "the Ruhr of Canada." The first described the shape (an irregular triangle bounded by the Seaway, the Richelieu River, and the New York boundary); the second, the economic character, heavy industry and chemicals. Old-established industries occupied the anchor-ends: shipbuilding at Sorel; textiles at Valleyfield.[3] Beside and between, new industries sprang up—chemicals, metal-fabricating and others.[4] Petroleum refining extended itself across the St. Lawrence from Montreal East to the South Shore (the region between Sorel and St. Lambert). The movement was stimulated by the construction of the oil pipeline from Portland, Maine. A vastly improved road and rail net and additional bridging drew both shores of the St. Lawrence together.

The new bridging was slanted toward road travel. When, in the late 1930's, the Mercier Bridge at Lachine was completed, the metropolitan area had two bridges for rail (the Victoria and the C.P.R. bridge at Lachine) and three (the Victoria, the Jacques Cartier, and the Mercier) for road traffic. The new bridging of the 1960's, the Champlain and the Sir Louis LaFontaine (a combination of bridge and tunnel), was entirely for road. The Victoria Bridge itself was reconstructed in order to increase its highway capacity. Montreal continued to be the major point for crossing the St. Lawrence. On the city or its immediate vicinity, converged the east-west Trans-Canada Highway and the north-south auto-routes, the Laurentides and the Cantons de l'Est.

Mass transit by electric train was a factor in the integration of the city and its southern frontier. As early as 1909, the Montreal & Southern Counties Railway provided the pioneer link, across the Victoria Bridge to St. Lambert. The following year, St. Lambert and Longueuil were connected. By 1916, the line from St. Lambert had reached Granby, almost fifty miles away. However, the Montreal and Southern Counties Railway ceased operation in October 1956. Ten years later, the subway (to be discussed in this chapter) was carried under the St. Lawrence to Longueuil. Bridges, tunnels, and road and rail connections made the metropolitan area one.

THE MODERN
MONTREALERS

Without people, the industrial transformation would have been impossible: Montreal would have been an ant-hill without ants. Population in the latest age was not merely large: it was diversified, versatile. The Montreal metropolitan area (the term was first employed officially in the Canadian Census of 1961) was estimated to contain about two-and-a-quarter million people. It included the Island of Montreal, Ile Jésus (to the north), and parts of the mainland, north as well as south. The City of Montreal had about one half of that total (1,191,062). In 1931 (the Census closest to the Diamond Jubilee of Confederation), there was no metropolitan area, and the population of the City of Montreal was just under 819,000. The 1961 figure placed Montreal well ahead of any other Canadian city, the sixth north of Mexico, and second only to Paris among the French cities of the world.

The grain of mustard seed to which Ville Marie was likened in 1642 had indeed grown—and retained its French savour. In 1961, French Canadians formed 66.5 per cent, that is about two thirds of the population. This was over five times the 12.4 per cent for the English, who, a hundred years before, had not only matched, but even exceeded the French in number (see Chapter 3). The change in their relative positions is one of the most striking features of Montreal's history since Confederation.

The English, with 147,686 (1961 Census), were simply the largest of a number of minority groups. Between 1951 and 1961, the Italians almost trebled their number and reached 79,841—well over half the English total. Then came Jews, 46,519; Poles, 17,210; Greeks, 15,471; Germans, 13,858; Hungarians, 10,304; Ukrainians, 9,199; and Russians, 7,726. Eight other European races, not listed individually, totalled 30,779. All Asiatic races together made up 8,000. By the centennial year, the term 'cosmopolitan', used earlier, really belonged to Montreal.

Modern Montreal presents a rich mosaic of peoples. The pattern is not very sharply cut, because there are few areas of the city that are the exclusive preserve of any one group. This is certainly true of the newer sections. The heavy immigration since World War II spread people all over Montreal. In the older parts of the city, certain sections were associated with certain peoples —the area south of St. Catherine and east of Bleury, with the Chinese; the area east of Park Avenue, with the Greeks. That the mosaic did not degenerate into a melting pot may be ascribed to the determination of Montrealers to be themselves. A paradox presents itself: the colony, the ghetto in the geographical sense, scarcely exists; the community, the cultural or kindred grouping flourishes. There are few cities in America where the geographical mingling of peoples has gone so far, and yet where the cultural identity is so vigorously maintained. Where but in Montreal could there be found a Nôtre Dame de Grâce kosher butcher shop?

Schooling was a continuing preoccupation, since Montreal experienced the vast child-population increase felt everywhere after the Second World War. Public schooling, traditionally administered on confessional lines (Roman Catholic and Protestant), each with its own curriculum, encountered great practical difficulties. "French-speaking Canadian" could no longer be equated with Roman Catholic; "English-speaking Canadian" with Protestant. English-speaking Roman Catholic children required instruction in English and in subjects that would admit them to English-language universities. Jewish children attended Protestant schools.

Solutions for problems such as these came slowly. In 1931, the Roman Catholic School Commission set up the first public English High School, D'Arcy McGee, and later developed an entire administrative office to care for the growing number of English Roman Catholic primary and secondary schools. In 1965, the first Jewish members were appointed to the Protestant Board of Greater Montreal. Sheer numbers posed their own problem. In 1942 (the centenary of its foundation), the Roman Catholic Commission cared for 100,000 children.[5] Thirty or so years later, the Commission was responsible for 205,000. It was the largest school-administering unit in Canada.

The independent or private school continued to form an important element in modern Montreal education. In an age of conformity and of monolithic organization, the independent school upheld the principle of free choice and of individual responsibility. Of the larger English-language independent schools, two, the Trafalgar School for Girls and Lower Canada College (known originally as the Church of St. John the Evangelist School), went back beyond 1900. One school, Miss Edgar's and Miss Cramp's, was pre-World War I (1909). Four, Selwyn House, the Study, the Weston School, and St. George's, were set up during or after the First World War. One, the Priory, was post-World War II.[6]

The strength of community loyalties was shown in schools. From the beginning of the twentieth century, Montreal Jews maintained schools for both secular and religious instruction. The Greek community also had its school. Its curriculum approximated to that of the Montreal Protestant Schools, but included instruction in religion and in Greek language and literature. The French colony maintained two schools, Collège Marie de France for girls, and Collège Stanislaus for boys. The curriculum of these schools was modelled on that of the *lycées* of France.

The universities shared in the general prosperity—and pressure. In 1943, the Université de Montréal moved to its current site, on the northern slopes of Mount Royal. There, satisfactory scope was found at last for the large student body and distinguished professoriate. The latter included such national, indeed international, figures as Mgr Olivier Maurault, historian and former *recteur,* and Hans Selye, Professor of Experimental Medicine. The Université de Montréal made an especial appeal to students from the French community in Africa and Asia. Like the great city of which it formed such a vital part, the Université de Montréal was itself cosmopolitan.

McGill University clung to its ancient site, since tradition and a sense of establishment were not easy to shake off. During the long principalship of F. Cyril

James (1940-63), imaginative advances were made. In 1948, a Faculty of Divinity was set up, staffed by the United and Anglican churches. It was hailed as the first co-operative of its kind in Canada. In reality, it was simply a modern expression of Protestantism's oldest tradition in Montreal, co-operation. A little later, the Islamic Institute brought to McGill scholars from parts of the world rarely visited by Montrealers. Doubtless the most widely known of McGill's efforts was the Montreal Neurological Institute, with its former director, Dr. Wilder Penfield.

In March 1948, Montreal's youngest university, Sir George Williams, came into being. For over two decades, as Sir George Williams College, it had been the educational arm of the Montreal YMCA.[7] The first great period of expansion came with the ending of the war and the flooding in of men and women from the armed services. The university rapidly outgrew its quarters in the Central YMCA. It outgrew new quarters constructed nearby. On the eve of the Centenary of Confederation, Sir George Williams University prepared to move into even newer quarters. Three moves in some fifteen years is an index of the pace of college growth. In spite of Sir George's development as a university, it maintained its high-school department. This, along with a night division of the university, continued to assist that part of the adult population for whom the YMCA classes were first established, over a century before. (See Chapter 8.)

A relative newcomer in the employment of evening classes for higher education was the Thomas More Institute. In 1945, it began in a modest way in downtown Montreal. By the centennial year, it had set up a suburban division as well. Its academic degrees are granted through the Univérsité de Montréal.

Modern Montrealers were primarily a family people. The newcomers, whether from other parts of Canada or from Europe, arrived as families or speedily established them. They were rooted; possessed of a sense of responsibility, in a way that the floating wartime population had not been. The ideals of suburbia invaded the city, even when the physical reality was only a duplex or an apartment. Prosperity made it possible to set high goals for children. Established position strengthened the desire to regain municipal independence, and to bring municipal services under public control. Education made Montrealers at once more critical and more able to act. Accompanying the dissatisfaction with the political scene, was a strong reaction against the open toleration of vice that had made Montreal's name a byword.

THE
CHURCH'S
ROLE

A powerful force also determined on reform was the Roman Catholic Church. It co-operated fully with the secular agencies, sustaining them by its influence on public opinion, and providing some of the most active leaders. The development of a vigorous, although unobtrusive, Roman Catholic social action was one of the outstanding features of the period.

The service was performed in spite of the heavy burden that the Church in Montreal was carrying. Within three weeks of the outbreak of war in 1939, Archbishop Bruchési died. For over twenty years he had been incapacitated by cruel disease. He was succeeded by the Most Reverend Georges Gauthier, who lived to enjoy the full dignity and title of Archbishop of Montreal for less than a year, after having served as Auxiliary Bishop and Archbishop since 1912. Very determined, possibly a little grim, Georges Gauthier had brought Montreal Roman Catholics through prosperity and depression, from war to war.[8]

In September 1940, the Right Reverend Joseph Charbonneau was consecrated Archbishop of Montreal. He had been Bishop of Hearst (in Northern Ontario) and Administrator of the Ottawa archdiocese, following the death of Archbishop Vachon. Charbonneau, therefore, brought considerable experience to the new task—the spiritual leadership of the largest and most complex Roman Catholic community in Canada. He was a commanding figure, tall and slender, the ideal

of the *Sacerdos Magnus*. The new Archbishop had the
satisfaction of opening the Université de Montréal on
its present site.[9] He had the problems and pains of
overseeing Montreal in the difficult war and post-war
years. He directed the settling of the refugees, especially the Poles and Hungarians. He took up the cudgels
in the interest of better housing. On him fell the care
of all the Roman Catholic churches of whatever language and tradition. The Archbishop showed great
awareness of new social conditions. He was deeply
distressed by the bitter industrial disputes of the
period, in particular the strike at Asbestos, in which
the resources of the government were thrown on the
side of management. In the early spring of 1950,
Joseph Charbonneau resigned the Montreal archdiocese. Reason of health was the official explanation.
Speculation had free rein. It was said that Charbonneau
was forced to resign. The ruling Union Nationale was
known to be hostile. Some of the Quebec bishops and
some of the religious orders were alleged to be critical
of him. Whatever the cause, Archbishop Charbonneau
retired to British Columbia, where he laboured in
humble chaplaincy posts at Victoria till his death
in 1959.[10]

His successor, Paul Emile Léger, was consecrated in
April 1950. He was a man of the most varied achievement. As a Sulpician, he was heir to the traditions of the
religious order that had been with Montreal since its beginning, over three hundred years before. He himself
had been a missionary and a director of missionary
studies in Japan. Since 1947, he had held a key post,
the Rectorship of the Canadian College in Rome. The
utmost efficiency had characterized all his administrations. No more than his predecessor was Archbishop
Léger prepared to tolerate the old ways, socially or
politically. In 1953, he was raised to the cardinalate,
under the title of Ste-Marie des Anges. He was the first
Montreal ecclesiastic to enjoy this signal honour. The
Cardinal took an active part in the Second Vatican
Council, and Montreal rejoiced in his eminence. Cardinal Léger possessed great receptivity, which, in turn,
influenced those who came close to him. Because of his
own experience, he had an understanding of adminis-

trative and governmental problems at all levels. His period of rule (1950-67) was fortunate for the secular reformers in Montreal. His loss was felt by the entire city, when he resigned as Archbishop in order to undertake missionary work among lepers in Africa.

MONTRÉAL
SOUS LE RÉGIME
DE LA PÈGRE

The secular reformers had encountered great difficulties. The effectiveness of the 1940 charter was compromised by the division of authority between mayor and chairman of the executive committee. From 1940 to 1944, Adhémar Raynault served two terms as mayor—that is, for the period of Camillien Houde's pèlerinage [pilgrimage], as he called his sojourn in the internment camp. On his release in 1944, Houde was promptly elected mayor, a feat he repeated in 1947 and 1950. In fact, in 1947 he was chosen by acclamation, a distinction that had eluded even Médéric Martin. (A referendum in 1944 lengthened the term for mayor and council to three years. For Houde's seventh and last term, that of 1950-54, the time was extended by another year.) In spite of his great popularity, Houde accomplished little. Drift rather than direction characterized his administrations—to the mounting irritation of the reform elements. The ninety-nine-man council was unwieldy and incapable of concerted action. That it would provide direction was hardly to be thought of. Conditions of war—the continuous movement of servicemen, a large floating population attracted by industry, and inadequate housing—made a situation that would have challenged the most efficient of city governments. Montreal's could scarcely qualify for that distinction.

In consequence, there was an orgy of commercialized vice on a scale seldom equalled. It took the forms principally of prostitution and gambling. Montreal had the highest venereal disease rate of any city in Canada. Since there were an estimated twelve thousand prostitutes, the incidence is not surprising. Gambling was described as one of the city's major industries. The financial returns were very impressive. One bookmaker and night club operator had an annual turnover of about two-and-a-half million dollars. While his expenses were proportionately high (his telephone bills over a two-year period were nearly $24,000) he was able to afford a fine residence in one of the more select suburbs. His experience may not have been entirely representative. Keepers of bawdy houses complained, "There's too much competition. Every second house of my street [is] a disorderly house." Another recalled the difficulties of getting started; she blamed competition and the high quality of her establishment. "[I kept] a very good house. We never opened on Good Friday."

The saturnalia continued long after the Second World War was over. This was shocking in itself. What was worse was the toleration shown. Among the owners (and profit-takers) of disorderly houses were a trust company, a bank, and a medical doctor; the latter, appropriately, a specialist in contagious diseases. The telephone and telegraph companies were implicated, since their services were employed in placing bets. Demoralization spread to the city administration. One of the gambling-house operators remarked: "The fines we paid took care of the Police Department salaries . . . and the city coffers were getting fat. I think that that is why we are tolerated." In face of this open toleration by the city itself, the dereliction of persons, policemen and others, seems trivial. There were, however, limits to toleration, even by the city administration. In 1947, a reform element in the council succeeded in having Pacifique Plante appointed to the police department as assistant director. Plante was a lawyer of wide experience, who had served the police as a legal adviser. He was very much in the main stream of the new reform. He was a graduate of St. Mary's College; one of his brothers was a Jesuit. Although he was dismissed from the police department in about a year's time, the investigations Plante had begun were continued. His revelations were printed in *Le Devoir* and later were published in book form, *Montréal sous le régime de la pègre.* Then followed a full judicial inquiry by Mr. Justice François Caron. Caron had two principal investigators, Plante and Jean Drapeau. The Caron report (1954) was a devastating indictment of more than a decade of social history. It brought to the final stage the political transformation of Montreal, because within three weeks of the release of the report, Jean Drapeau was swept into the mayoralty of Montreal.

The tone of the civic election of October 1954 had an obvious antecedent—the recently concluded Caron vice probe. The connection was underscored by the principals in the election, Camillien Houde and Jean Drapeau. Houde had been mayor since 1944, in other words for much of the period covered by the probe. Although he had not been touched by any of the charges, Houde had shown himself to be conspicuously insensitive. He had refused to appear before Mr. Justice Caron to give evidence. Worse than that was his characterization of the probe: it was "an attempt at vengeance by one group against another. They are trying to dig up some mud and throw it at us, and we will try to throw it right back." This gratuitous aligning of himself with the discredited old order was simply an index of Houde's inability to grasp the temper of the times. He had been outdated.

It was more than the outdating of a man. There had been a Houde era. In it Montreal had lost much of its earlier individuality and had come to resemble other great American cities. The population, essentially nomadic, moved into, out of, and within the city. Having no roots, the Montreal population had no sense of the past and could learn nothing from the past. A further factor had been the very large number of unskilled and unorganized wage-earners. They crowded into the service occupations in which there was little permanence.[11] Camillien Houde had fitted easily into this setting. He too had moved from job to job.

Houde's municipal career had only a superficial consistency. It was broken by excursions into provincial and federal politics. As mayor, Houde looked for, rather than made, opportunities. Like his debonair counterpart, Jimmy Walker of New York, Houde was essentially the showman. His presence was enough to guarantee the success of any gathering. The exercise of this talent, rather than anything more serious, became the hallmark of the Houde administrations between 1944 and 1954. Urgent civic problems, chaos in transportation and mounting crime, were neglected. The price that Médéric Martin paid for passivity in 1928 was paid by Camillien Houde in 1954. Houde died in 1957.

THE FIRST DRAPEAU ADMINISTRATION

The reason for the choice of Jean Drapeau as candidate may not have been clear to the general public. True, he had been one of the investigators, along with Plante, under Caron. He had not been accorded, probably because he had not sought it, the personal identification of his more flamboyant colleague. This very lack of conspicuous involvement may have been a recommendation. It appears to have appealed strongly to Pierre DesMarais and to other reformers on the Montreal city council.[12] DesMarais had been a councillor and a member of the executive committee for a long period, first as an ally and then as an opponent of J. O. Asselin, the committee's most significant chairman. More recently, DesMarais had founded the *Ligue d'action civique,* the political arm of the reformers. DesMarais had been instrumental in bringing on the Caron inquiry. In 1950, he had refused to vote the police estimates until the charges publicized by Plante were thoroughly investigated.

DesMarais's determination to back Drapeau was decisive. It brought into effective alliance the political reformer and the political idealist. The element of idealism was part of Drapeau long before 1954. Twelve years earlier he had been one of the younger men who founded the *Ligue pour la défense du Canada,* and, later, the *Bloc populaire.* These were groups that had been formed to oppose conscription for overseas service, or, more accurately, to oppose conscription as the only means to raise men for overseas service.

New York City. From planning to completion, imported conceptions dominated. The new Montreal bore virtually no resemblance to its historic self.

From 1958, the physical transformation went on rapidly. To the west of Place Ville Marie, the Canadian Imperial Bank of Commerce building rose to a height of forty-three storeys (604 feet). Its construction involved the razing of the more attractive part of the Windsor Hotel, and with it so many memories of nineteenth-century Montreal. Seven other major buildings were erected along Dorchester Street, Windsor Street, Victoria Square, and Place d'Armes. The transformation spread to other parts of the city, although without the dramatic effects produced in the central area. Old landmarks vanished, obliterated or overtopped and hidden by the new growth. So widespread was their destruction, that in 1962 the city and province set up the Viger Commission in order to salvage what it could of oldest Montreal. An area between Notre Dame and St. Paul streets east of Place d'Armes was designated as an historic site, where further demolition was forbidden. Even Mount Royal, Montreal's oldest landmark, was in danger of being lost among buildings that crowded its slopes, and skyscrapers that rose from its base. The cross on the mountain, put up in 1924 to commemorate the one carried by Maisonneuve in 1643, was also in danger of being lost—overtopped by the television towers erected in 1952.

The extensive building had the most diverse consequences. The boon to industry and employment was very great. (It was estimated that for every man working on construction, ten were employed in auxiliary trades.) The provision of ample office space meant that Montreal would become increasingly a city for headquarters or main offices. On the other hand, the social structure of large parts of Montreal was completely dislocated. The new buildings sharpened the already acute problem of movement. The congestion of people and vehicles round the new buildings threatened to produce immobility. The replanning of old streets and the opening of new ones were certainly beneficial—as the experiment made with Dorchester Street showed. The long-range solution was the decentralizing of many phases of city life and the placing of public transportation below ground.

DECENTRALIZATION AND URBAN TRANSPORTATION

Decentralization of the residential area was an old story. In the 1950's it was assisted by the universality of the automobile. The car was not the original cause. Dissatisfaction with city living long antedated it. The automobile simply expanded the distance to which city workers could retreat at the end of their day. Montreal spread and suburbs spread outside Montreal. Together they formed a metropolitan area. Decentralizing business was less easy. Retailers, however, quickly followed the outward movement of population. Supermarkets (the term was synonymous with self-service food stores) came first in the 1930's, with the introduction of packaged foods. In 1953 and 1954, the first shopping centres were laid out, one on the eastern border of the city, at Pie IX and Jean Talon; the other, far beyond the western limits, at Dorval. In both, Henry Morgan, Montreal's oldest department store took the initiative.[14]

The placing of public transportation underground was a difficult matter. As far back as 1910, a subway had been projected. Even in the projection, however, Montreal was far behind Boston and New York, which themselves were about half a century behind London. Montreal's subway remained in the planning stage for over fifty years. This was scarcely a matter for congratulation, in view of the discomfort of Montreal weather and the extreme dilatoriness of Montreal traffic. In 1953, however, the Transportation Commission (the public authority that in 1950 had taken over from the Tramways Company) recommended the first unit of a subway system. Construction was begun in May 1962, with an opening goal of 1966—a goal that was reached in October of that year. It was to consist, initially, of a north-south and an east-west line. Features of the Paris Métro, for example, rubber-tired rolling stock, were to be incorporated. The name métro (or metro) was also borrowed. The larger plan contemplated extending the subway to serve all Montreal and to integrate the tunnel railway under Mount Royal. With these additions, Montreal may well claim victory over its size, its situation, and even its weather.

LE PARTI CIVIQUE

The defeat of Jean Drapeau in 1957 was less disastrous than might appear. The *Ligue d'action civique* had elected a majority of the councillors. The new mayor, Sarto Fournier, had difficulty in seating his choice as chairman of the executive committee. In the council, DesMarais made himself the leader of an organized opposition. Fournier's following was made up of the most diverse elements. He himself was a federal Liberal senator. Nevertheless, he had the tacit support of the Union Nationale. The *Ralliement de grand Montréal,* as Fournier's party was named, was not much more than a hold-all for groups opposed to Drapeau. Drapeau himself was not disposed to sulk. He launched out on a Quebec-wide promotional tour. He was an accomplished platform speaker; his discourses a judicious blend of civic virtue ("Pourqoui avoir peur?" and "Trente pièces d'argent") and French-Canadian nationalism ("Elizabeth ou Maisonneuve?" and "Abbatre le régime et changer le système"). Gradually, he drew out a new tactic. His convictions were expressed at a later time to an English-speaking admirer: "I had been very naive. I realized that I had not run my affairs like a good politician. . . . The next time I would produce a firm programme, a city-wide body of candidates, . . . and if elected would form a government instead of a council of individuals." [15] Drapeau executed his plans with despatch. He formed his own party, the *Parti civique,* although this involved a break with the *Ligue d'action civique,* and with its leader, Pierre DesMarais. The second-in-command of the new party was Lucien Saulnier, a businessman who was to display marked talents as a civic administrator.

In the elections of October 1960, the *Parti civique* won a clear mandate. It carried forty-six of the sixty-six council seats open to contest. A referendum abolished A and C categories of councillors and thus made the votes of all citizens equal. Drapeau was swept into the mayoralty with a majority of thirty thousand. The new administration set its house in order. Lucien Saulnier became chairman of the executive committee. Mayor and chairman worked in harmony, imposing their program on the council through the disciplined *Parti civique.*

The fortunes of the new Montreal régime were greatly improved by the only slightly less new régime at Quebec. The Lesage government showed itself sympathetic towards the program of Drapeau and the *Parti civique.* A commission, usually called the Champagne Commission from the name of its chairman, made its final report in 1961. It recommended a form of municipal administration closely resembling the type towards which Jean Drapeau was moving. The council was to be remodelled to form a parliament. The executive committee was to become a cabinet. Essential to the effective working of the plan were municipal political parties with their recognized leaders and programs: "Le chef du parti victorieux devient le chef de l'administration et il lui appartient de désigner les membres de son comité [executive committee] parmi les conseilliers élus par son parti." The Commission broke with its own logic, however, by recommending, also, the continuation of the office of mayor and the filling of it by conventional election from the city at large. At the next election, therefore, Jean Drapeau found himself once more Mayor—not the first Premier —of Montreal. The form of government set up in virtue of the Champagne Commission is usually described as a parliamentary administration. In reality, it was far from being so. The continuation of the mayoralty as an independently elected office warped the analogy. There were other departures, although the more important of these were in convention rather than in constitution. There was, for example, no clearly defined opposition party or leader.

When the Champagne Commission made its preliminary report, shortly before the 1960 elections, it recommended that the incoming mayor and council should hold office for only two years. Therefore elections were held next in October 1962. At the same time, a referendum again lengthened the term of office, this time to four years. The *Parti civique* won its second victory; Drapeau, his third. Progress was rapid: in 1962, contracts for the first section of the subway were let. In 1963, the Place des Arts was opened. In 1964, the site for Expo 67 was turned over by the city to the federal authority responsible for running the Fair. Equally impressive was the smooth operation of the council itself. The majority enjoyed by the *Parti civique* ensured the easy passage of legislation introduced by the Executive Committee. The system was markedly flexible. When, in the autumn of 1961, the subway was under discussion, the council chamber was transformed into a lecture hall, complete with charts, plans, and maps. As the centenary of Confederation approached, it looked very much as if a definite answer had been given to the old conundrum, can Montreal be governed?

EXPO 67

The most glittering of all the transformations were those connected with Expo 67.[16] In this instance, the quiet and park-like St. Helen's Island and the shallows lying to the south and west were turned into the site of the sixth International Exhibition. The shallows were filled in to form an artificial island that extended along the Seaway the full distance between the Victoria and Jacques Cartier bridges. The creation was given the name "Ile Notre-Dame." St. Helen's Island itself was enlarged to include two small downstream islands. A third part of the site was on the mainland, where the

Mackay pier was transformed into the Cité du Havre. On these areas, partly natural, partly artificial, were erected the structures intended to give expression to the Expo theme, Man and his World.

Expo 67 was the popular name given to the Universal and International Exhibition of 1967. It was the first official first-category world exhibition to be held in the western hemisphere. The terms "first category" and "exhibition" have special meaning in the definitions provided by the International Bureau of Exhibitions, under whose authority Expo was held. According to these definitions, there were previously only two first-category world exhibitions, those held in 1935 and 1958 at Brussels in Belgium.

Montreal had participated in world fairs from their beginning, having sent articles to the two earliest—that of London in 1851 and that of Paris, 1855-56. Between 1850 and 1897, Montreal had been the scene of some twenty-two or twenty-three exhibitions on a country-wide scale. Some were in the nature of agricultural fairs; others, of a more general character. That of 1868 was advertised as "Military and Industrial." However, Montreal had withdrawn and left the field to Toronto, which in 1878 organized the annual Canadian National Exhibition.[17]

In 1895, Montreal's claim to play host internationally had been promoted by the newspaper press, and based upon the beauty of the site the city could offer—St. Helen's Island: "une autre Venise transportée au milieu du St-Laurent . . . idée irrésistiblement séductrice . . . site ravissant."

Montreal's failure to be host at a national exhibition on Canada's fiftieth anniversary was not the result of anyone's choice. The proposal was made in the federal parliament in March 1914, by the Honourable Rodolphe Lemieux, but when the Golden Jubilee date rolled round, in 1917, Montrealers had other things to think about.

In 1937, Adhémar Raynault, then serving his first term as mayor, put forward plans for again trying to make Montreal the site of an international exhibition. It would mark the founding of the city. But when 1942 came, Montrealers were preoccupied (as they had been in 1917) with something much more pressing.

Later mayors were more fortunate. The proposals that actually secured Expo 67 for Montreal were begun under Sarto Fournier and completed under Jean Drapeau. "Under" is too weak a term to describe the involvement of Jean Drapeau. Following his election (for his second term) in 1960, he took up the Expo proposition in a decisive fashion. To say that he made it a Drapeau show is hardly fair to others or to Jean Drapeau himself; but he certainly made securing the world exhibition very much his own cause. The favourable decision, rendered in November 1962 by the International Bureau of Expositions, was in the nature of a personal triumph. However, Drapeau had many more plans for Montreal, plans of far greater consequence than even that of playing host on an international scale.

Five years, 1962-67, were scant time for planning. A site and its preparation were the first necessities. These were secured by Montreal on St. Helen's Island and Ile Notre-Dame. In 1964, the city transferred the site to the Crown corporation charged with the supervision of the exhibition. The ceremony, the *nuit des îles,* was performed on the night of June 30 - July 1. It was a brilliant spectacle—in spite of the dramatic unco-operativeness of the weather. About nine months later, there was another ceremony, the carrying of a torch from Ottawa to light the Expo flame, a forceful reminder that just two years remained before the official opening, April 28, 1967.

As this date approached, Expo 67 underwent its final transformation, from paper plans to realization in metals, concrete, and plastics. The theme, Man and his World, put a premium on the present and the future. It also put a premium on science and culture. The physical expression of the theme challenged the imagination of the architects of the pavilions and the designers of their interiors. Colour was also effectively employed to touch senses not much affected by form. Seventy nations participated, either in their own buildings or those that were shared. Sharing was carried furthest, as was appropriate, in the Christian Pavilion, a co-operative effort by the major Canadian churches. Since it was recognized that no gathering, however improving, could succeed without fun, a special section of Expo, La Ronde, was set aside for amusement. Also provided nearby was a mooring-place for pleasure craft, since it was expected that many patrons would arrive by water. This was one of the points at which history and the modernity of Expo met. The founders of Montreal three hundred and twenty-five years ago came by the river; and it was the river that was the favoured means of travel of the Fathers of Confederation one hundred years ago.

Expo fully justified the careful preparations. Its six months' run, April 28 to October 29, was a resounding success. Attendance passed the fifty million mark. (The official total for the 185 days was 50,306,648.) Everyone found something worthwhile, for the hallmark was variety. Paralleling the physical display was one of cultural entertainment, known as the World Festival. It was not restricted to the main Expo site, but extended into Montreal, where the World Exhibition rented the Place des Arts. (Connection between the city and island sites was provided by both surface and subway routes.) Expo 67 was the most international of exhibitions yet held. It enabled Montrealers to see people from all over the world, and it enabled people from all over the world to see Montreal. It was entirely fitting that the best view of the modern city could be had from the site of Expo 67.

The transformations made in Montreal since the end of the Second World War were something more than the accomplishment of a party, let alone of a single individual. They sprang from the social evolution of Montreal itself in the most recent period.

The ground swell of social change set in with the early years of the present century. A new class, for lack of a more accurate term described as a middle class, spread over the city. The process was far from rapid. The First World War, as was suggested in the chapter "1914 and Afterwards," was a delaying factor; so, also, the depression decade of the 1930's. The Second World War, however, completed the victory of the new order. By this period, other factors were taking effect. The general rise of income and the levelling up of educational opportunities had greatly enlarged the middle class. Indeed, it was no longer a middle class, since the opportunities of the modern period blurred the old social lines and facilitated the rise (and secured the ready acceptance) of competent newcomers. All this was far from constituting a social revolution, yet it placed the reality of power with the great mass of Montrealers whose fortunes lay between the two extremes of wealth and poverty.

While poverty and slum conditions certainly were to be found, they were no longer accepted as preordained parts of the social order. The slums were undergoing change. The Jeanne Mance rehousing project had placed blocks of moderately priced apartments in the dying area east of St. Lawrence Boulevard. A corresponding development was planned for the southwest section of the city. The chief victims of poverty were individuals, who through age, sickness, or lack of skills were unable to claim their share of the general prosperity. The rehabilitation of human beings requires more delicate forms of treatment, and it would be rash indeed to claim that Montreal possesses all the answers to the most pressing problem of the modern western world. The history of Montreal since the Second World War has been the history of all its people; not merely the history of a political nation or of an exploiting class.

The main stream of Montreal's philosophy was derived from social forces and ideals generated within itself. The chief source was its preponderant French-Canadian citizens. In its most modern period, the descendants of the founders of Montreal were its masters. Responsibility for good government was theirs. It is a fair assumption that much of the determination that inspired the DesMarais-Drapeau-Saulnier reformation came from the patriotic resolve to make the French-Canadian name shine in metropolitan administration.[18]

NOTES TO CHAPTERS

CHAPTER 1: EARLY MONTREAL 1642-1817

1. The earliest writings dealing with Montreal may be consulted in modern editions:

H. P. BIGGAR,
The Voyages of Jacques Cartier
(Ottawa: Public Archives of Canada, 1924);

H. P. BIGGAR and Others (editors),
The Works of Samuel de Champlain
(6 vols.; Toronto: The Champlain Society, 1922-32), vol. III;

RALPH FLENLEY (translator and editor) DOLLIER DE CASSON,
A History of Montreal 1640-1672
(Toronto: J. M. Dent and Sons, 1928).

2. E. R. ADAIR,
"The Evolution of Montreal under the French Regime,"
Canadian Historical Association, Annual Report 1942, pp. 20-41; also,

G. LANCTOT, *Montréal au temps de la Nouvelle France*
("Bibliothèque d'histoire scientifique"; Montreal: G. Ducharme, 1942).

3. A. L. BURT,
The Old Province of Quebec
(Toronto: Ryerson Press, 1933), chap. 1; also,

G. LANCTOT,
Histoire du Canada (3 vols.; Montréal: Beauchemin, 1962-65), vol. 111, chap. 8.

4. B. G. SACK,
History of the Jews in Canada
(2 vols.; Montreal: Canadian Jewish Congress, 1935), vol. 1, chap. 5.

5. "Copy of the Register of the Parish of Montreal, 1766-1789,"
Report of the Public Archives of Canada (Ottawa, 1885); also,

J. I. COOPER,
The Blessed Communion
(Montreal: Diocese of Montreal, 1960), chap. 1.

6. H.-A. VERREAU,
L'invasion du Canada: collection des mémoires (Montréal: E. Senécal, 1873); also, J.-J. Lefebvre, "Les Canadiens-Français et la Révolution américaine," *Le Societé historique franco-américaine* (Boston, 1949).

7. J. H. SMITH,
Our Struggle for the Fourteenth Colony (2 vols.; New York: G. P. Putnam, 1907), vol. I, chap. 16 and vol. II, chap. 1.

8. R. CAMPBELL,
A History of the Scotch Presbyterian Church in St. Gabrie Street (Montreal: W. Drysdale, 1887); also,

E. A. McDOUGALL,
"The American Element in the Early Presbyterian Church in Montreal" (McGill University thesis, 1965).

CHAPTER 2: HOPES RAISED BY STEAM

1. M. I. NEWBIGIN,
Canada, The Great River, The Lands and the Men (London: Christophers, 1926).

2. G. J. J. TULCHINSKY,
"The Lachine Canal" (McGill University thesis, 1960).

3. "View of the Harbour of Montreal," engraved by R. E. Sproule (Montreal: A. Bourne, 1830).

4. N. T. CORLEY,
"The Montreal Ship Channel, 1805-1865" (McGill University thesis, 1961).

5. G. H. Wilson, "The Application of Steam Navigation to the St. Lawrence 1809-1840" (McGill University thesis, 1961).

6. J. HODGES,
The Construction of the Great Victoria Bridge (London: J. Weale, 1860).

7. T. C. KEEFER,
"Travel and Transportation,"
Eighty Years of Progress in British North America, ed. H. Y. Hind (Toronto: Stebbins, 1863), pp. 90-255.

8. W. H. ATHERTON,
History of the Harbour Front of Montreal (Montreal: City Improvement League, 1935).

9. John Fotheringham diary, various entries in the 1850's; private possession.

CHAPTER 3: NINETEENTH-CENTURY MONTREAL

1. LEON POULIOT,
Monseigneur Bourget et son temps (2 vols.; Montréal: Beauchemin, 1955-56), vol. I, *Les années de préparation.*

2. H. E. MacDERMOT,
A History of the Montreal General Hospital (Montreal: Montreal General Hospital, 1950).

3. REXFORD, GEMMELL, McBAIN,
The History of the High School of Montreal (Montreal: privately printed, n.d.).

4. *Le diocese de Montréal à la fin du dix-neuvieme siecle,* ed. R. Bellemare (Montréal: E. Senécal, 1900), pp. 40-56.

5. R. TANGHE,
"La population," *Montréal Economique,* ed. Esdras Minville (Montréal: Editions Fides, 1943), chap. 3, p. 100.

CHAPTER 4: MUNICIPAL GOVERNMENT, PART 1

1. E.-Z. MASSICOTTE,
Repertoire des arrets, édits, ordonnances etc. conservés dans les archives du Palais de Justice de Montréal (Montréal: G. Ducharme, libraire-éditeur, 1919).

2. The minutes of the Session of the Peace are to be found in the Judicial Archives of the District of Montreal, Old Court House; those of the Magistrates, in the Archives of the City of Montreal, City Hall.

3. Séssion de la paix, le 6 novembre, 1826.

4. J.-C. LAMOTHE,
Histoire de la corporation de la cité de Montréal (Montréal: Montreal Printing and Publishing Co., 1903), chap. 12.

5. This was common experience in older Canadian cities.
Vide, D. C. MASTERS,
The Rise of Toronto (Toronto: University of Toronto Press, 1947), chap. 2 and 3; also,

J. E. MIDDLETON,
Toronto's Hundred Years (Toronto: Centennial Committee, 1934).

CHAPTER 5: ON THE EVE OF CONFEDERATION

1. *Montreal in 1856* (Montreal: Grand Trunk . . . Celebration Committee, 1856); a valuable industrial survey.

2. F. D. ADAMS, *A History of Christ Church Cathedral, Montreal* (Montreal: Burton, 1941), chap. 5.

3. *The Montreal Gazette,* November 11, 1860.

4. *Colonial Church and School Society, Montreal Committee Report* (Montreal, 1860); also,
W. SIEBERT,
The Underground Railroad (New York: The Macmillan Company, 1899), chap. 7; also,
W. SIEBERT,
Vermont's Underground Railroad and Anti-Slavery Record (Columbus, Ohio: Spahr and Glenn, 1937).

5. The Montreal press covered the memorial services very fully. The press was united in denouncing the assassination of Lincoln. It had been greatly divided in its opinion of the War: Conservative opinion favoured the South; Reform, the North.

CHAPTER 6: MONTREAL AND CONFEDERATION

1. The fullest newspaper accounts of the first Dominion Day celebrations were provided by *La Minerve* and *The Gazette*.

2. G. E. CLERK;
diary, various entries, 1866 and 1867; private possession.

3. Quoted by Peter Waite, *The Life and Times of Confederation* (Toronto: University of Toronto Press, 1962), p. 135.

4. JOHN WOOD,
Memoir of Henry Wilkes, D.D., L.L.D. (Montreal: F. E. Grafton and Sons, 1887), p.194.

5. JOSEPH DESJARDINS,
Guide parlementaire historique de la province de Quebéc (Québec: Bibliothèque législative, 1902).

6. JOSEPH TASSE (ed.),
Discours de l'Hon. G. E. Cartier etc. (Montreal: E. Senécal, 1893, pp. 399-408, "Au banquet offert aux délégués de la conférence de Québec à Montréal, le octobre 1864").

CHAPTER 7: ACROSS THE CONTINENT AND BEYOND

1. JOHN BOYD, *Sir George E. Cartier Bart.* (Toronto: The Macmillan Company, 1914), chap. 15.

2. G. F. G. STANLEY,
The Birth of Western Canada (Toronto: Oxford University Press, 1960), chap. 7; also BOYD and GLAZEBROOK.

3. G. de T. GLAZEBROOK,
History of Transportation in Canada (Toronto: Ryerson, 1936), sect. VII, chap. 3 and 4.

4. R. R. BROWN,
"The Ice Railway," *Bulletin of the Canadian Railway Historical Association* (Montreal, 1960).

5. The standard biographies of Lord Strathcona,

W. T. R. PRESTON,
Life and Times of Lord Strathcona (London: Eveleigh Nash, 1914), and

BECKLES WILLSON,
Life of Lord Strathcona and Mount Royal (London: Cassells, 1914), are not very helpful with regard to his business life. More useful references are provided in

J MURRAY GIBBON,
Steel of Empire (Indianapolis: Bobbs Merrill, 1935).

6. J. MURRAY GIBBON,
chap. 17, p. 210 ff.

7. O. LAVALLEE,
"Windsor Station, 1889-1964," *Canadian Rail* (Feb. 1964), no. 152.

8. B. A. McKELVIE,
Pageant of B.C. (Toronto: Nelson, 1957), chap. 98.

CHAPTER 8: O GOD! O MONTREAL!

1. O. MAURAULT,
Grand Séminaire de Montréal
(Montréal : Grand Séminaire,
1940).

2. O. MAURAULT, "L'Université
de Montréal," *Cahiers des Dix*
(Montréal, 1952), vol. XVII.

3. T. P. SLATTERY, *Loyola and
Montreal* (Montreal : Palm
Publishers, 1962), chap. 5.

4. P. DESJARDINS,
*Le Collège Sainte-Marie de
Montréal* (Montréal : Collège
Ste-Marie, 1942), pt. 1, chap. 2.

5. REXFORD, GEMMELL, and
McBAIN, *History of the High
School of Montreal* (Montreal,
privately printed, n.d.).

6. G. M. BURDETT, "The High
School for Girls, 1875-1914"
(McGill University thesis, 1963).

7. K. D. HUNTE, "The Develop-
ment of the System of Education
in Canada East, 1841-1867"
(McGill University thesis, 1962) ;
K. D. HUNTE,
"The Ministry of Public Instruction
in Quebec, 1867-1875" (McGill
University thesis, 1964).

8. M. CYRILLE, "Les Frères des
Ecoles chrètiennes," *L'Ecole
canadienne* (Montréal :
Commission des écoles
catholiques de Montréal, 1942),
pp. 50-54.

9. W. P. PERCIVAL,
Across the Years
(Montreal : Gazette Publising
Company, 1946), chap. 2.

10. HENRY MOTT
manuscripts, Redpath Library,
McGill University.

11. *Mechanics Institute of
Montreal* (Montreal : Mechanics
Institute, 1940).

12. *Annuaire de l'institut
canadien pour l'année 1866*
(Montréal, 1866).

13. H. C. CROSS,
*One Hundred Years of Service
with Youth* (Montreal : YMCA
Central Board, 1951), pp. 131-4.

14. *Art Association of Montreal,*
annual reports, various dates
1874-92. The Association's act of
incorporation specified that "a
school of design" was among its
objectives. The Montreal
Association of Artists, formed in
1847, encouraged individual
members to take pupils.

15. *A Tradition Lives: The Story
of the Gazette* (Montreal : Gazette
Publishing Company, 1963).

16. GEORGE MURRAY,
"A Notable Journalistic Career,"
Canadian Magazine, vol. XXXII
(no. 5, March, 1909), pp. 417-21.
This appears to be the ealiest
appreciation of the *Star* and its
founder. It contains all the legends
repeated at later times.

17. AMY REDPATH
diary. Redpath Library, McGill
University.

18. MAURAULT,
Grand Séminaire, "Nos anciens."

CHAPTER 9: THE POST-CONFEDERATION CITY

1. Census of Canada, 1871 and
1881 ; annual reports of the City
of Montreal ; Lovell's Montreal
directories.

2. A. R. GEORGE,
The House of Birks (Montreal :
privately printed, 1946).

3. R. BELLEMARE (ed.)
*Le diocese de Montréal à la fin du
dix-neuvieme siecle* (Montréal :
1900, E. Senécal), pp. 80-83.

4. *The Centenary of the Montreal
Board of Trade* (Montreal : Board
of Trade, 1922).

5. *Histoire du commerce
canadien-francais de Montréal*
(Montréal : La Chambre de
Commerce, 1894), pp. 79-96.

6. S. A. AYER,
"The Locomotive Engineers'
Strike on the Grand Trunk
Railway" (McGill University thesis,
1961).

7. J. I. COOPER,
History of the Montreal Hunt
(Montreal : privately printed,
1954).

CHAPTER 10: THE CITY BELOW THE HILL

1. *Royal Commission on the Relations of Capital and Labour* (3 vols.; Ottawa: Queen's Printer, 1889), vol. 3, "Evidence—Quebec part 1").

2. W. KILBOURN, *The Elements Combined* (Toronto: Clarke-Irwin, 1962), p. 26.

3. R. RUMILLY, *Histoire de la Province de Québec* (Montréal: B. Valiquette, 1941), vol. 1, *Georges-Etienne Cartier*, p. 103.

4. V. O. CHAN, "The Canadian Knights of Labour" (McGill University thesis, 1949).

5. S. A. AYER, "The Locomotive Engineers' Strike on the Grand Trunk Railway" (McGill University thesis, 1961).

6. A. E. AMES, manuscript collection, Redpath Library, McGill University.

7. City of Montreal annual reports, Department of Health.

8. J. C. LAMOTHE, *Histoire de la corporation de la cité de Montréal* (Montréal: Montreal Printing and Publishing Company, 1903), pp. 260-329 and 332-408.

9. A. D. HART (ed.), *The Jew in Canada* (Montreal and Toronto: Jewish Publications Ltd., 1926). chap. 2; also

B. G. SACK, *History of the Jews in Canada* (2 vols.; Montreal: Canadian Jewish Congress, 1945), vol. I, chaps. 17 and 19.

CHAPTER 11: MUNICIPAL GOVERNMENT, PART 2

1. J.-C. LAMOTHE, *Histoire de la corporation de la cité de Montréal* (Montréal: Montreal Printing and Publishing Company, 1903), "La galèrie des maires," pp. 306-7.

2. *Ibid.* pp. 442-612, "La galèrie des fonctionnaires municipaux."

3. Discussion became less insistent in the later 1850's, when the cost of the municipalization of water service was counted.

4. The City Passenger Railway and later the City Street Railway were important factors in the fortunes of a number of municipal figures. Préfontaine was virtually the Passenger Railway's advocate in the council.

5. In his Montreal direcotry of 1871-72, John Lovell introduced "an improvement." He provided separate listings of names for the surrounding municipalities. The new arrangement indicated the growing importance of the nearby towns.

CHAPTER 12: TRANSPORT, COMMUNICATIONS, POWER

1. G. R. STEVENS,
The Canadian National Railways
(2 vols.; Toronto: Clarke-Irwin,
1961), vol. I, sect. 1, "The
Lachine Railway," pp. 33-39; also
*Railway and Locomotive
Historical Society Bull. 39*
(March 1936), chap. 6, "The
Champlain and St. Lawrence
Railway."

2. O. LAVALLEE,
*The City Passenger Railway
Company* (Montreal: Canadian
Railway Historical Association,
1961).

3. *Urban Transportation in
Montreal, 1861-1961* (Montreal:
Transportation Commission, 1961).

4. HENRY MOTT,
manuscript collection; Redpath
Library, McGill University.

5. W. H. ATHERTON, *History of
Montreal* (3 vols.; Montreal:
S. J. Clarke Publishing Co., 1914),
vol. II, pp. 403-4.

6. HENRY MOTT,
manuscript collection; Redpath
Library, McGill University.

7. Montreal newspapers,
September 1891.

8. *Histoire du commerce
canadien-francaise de Montréal,*
(Montréal: La chambre de
commerce, 1894), "Biographies et
Portraits," p. 115.

CHAPTER 13: THE ERA OF CONSOLIDATION

1. Between 1892 and 1898.
Lovell's Montreal directories
contained valuable business
summaries. Similar ones appeared
irregularly at later times.

2. *Urban Transportation in
Montreal, 1861-1961* (Montreal:
Tranportation Commission, 1961).

3. R. M. BINNS, "The Black Cars,"
Canadian Rail (February, 1966),
No. 174, pp. 27-31.

4. "Special Historical Supplement:
Sketch of the Royal Bank of
Canada," *Canadian Annual
Review*, 1910, pp. 73-82.

5. C. BERIGTHON,
*The Canadian Stock Exchange,
with Special Reference to the
Montreal Stock Exchange*
(Montreal: privately printed,
1940); also,

J. S. JOHNSON,
"History and Organization of the
Montreal Stock Exchange"
(McGill University thesis, 1934).

6. T. DRIBERG,
Lord Beaverrbook (London:

Weidenfeld and Nicolson, 1956);
also,

F. A. MACKENZIE, *Beaverbrook,
an Authentic Biography* (London:
Jarrolds, 1931).

7. LORD BEAVERBROOK,
"My Early Life," *Atlantic Advocate*
February-August 1964 (Fifth
Instalment, June 1964), vol. LIV,
no. 10.

8. R. RUMILLY, *Histoire de la
Province de Quebéc* (Montréal:
Valiquette, 1944), vol. XIII,
Henri Bourassa, pp. 114-6.

9. "Discours de Henri Bourassa,"
Le Devoir le 14 janvier 1914.

10. J. H. DALES,
*Hydroelectricity and Industrial
Development in Quebec*
(Cambridge: Harvard University
Press, 1957).

11. *Histoire du commerce
canadien-francaise de Montréal*
(Montréal: La chambre de
commerce, 1894), "Biographies et
Portraits," p. 101.

CHAPTER 14: THE EARLY TWENTIETH CENTURY

1. The air meets were fully reported in the contemporary Montreal press. For a modern account, *vide*

F. H. ELLIS, *Canada's Flying Heritage* (Toronto: University of Toronto Press, 1954), Chaps. 7 and 9.

2. L. G. REYNOLDS, *The British Immigrant* (Toronto: Oxford University Press, 1935), pt. II, chap. 4.

3. A. D. HART (ed.), *The Jew in Canada* (Toronto and Montreal: Jewish Publications Ltd., 1926; also,

JUDITH SEIDEL "The Development and Social Adjustment of the Jewish Community in Montreal" (McGill University thesis, 1935).

4. The earliest Montreal directory was published by Thomas Doige in 1819. Robert Mackay began issuing his directory in 1842. This was continued by his widow and later by John Lovell.

5. ROBERT GEORGE, *The House of Birks* (Montreal: privately published 1946), pp. 19-22.

6 HENRY MOTT manuscrtpt collection, Redpath Library

McGill University.

7. "Montreal To-Day," *Montreal Herald,* September 13-20, 1909.

8. E.-J. AUCLAIR, *Saint-Henri des tanneries* (Montréal: Imprimerie de la Salle, 1942), and

E.-Z. MASSICOTTE, *La Cité de Sainte-Cunégonde* Montréal: J.-S. Houle, 1893).

9. Information supplied by the City of Westmount.

10. This date is two years earlier than that of the beginning of municipal electrical generation at Sherbrooke. *Vide*

R. RUMILLY, *Histoire de la Province de Quebec,* vol. XIII, *Henri Bourassa,* p. 125.

11. L. G. REYNOLDS, *British Immigrant,* pp. 118-20 and 140-44.

12. D. GIROUARD, *Lake St. Louis* (Montréal: Poirier and Bisette, 1893), pp. 233-43.

13. ANTHONY CLEGG, *The Mount Royal Tunnel* (Montreal: Canadian Railway Historical Association, 1963), chap. 2.

14. *Le Devoir,* le 10 janvie r 1910

CHAPTER 15: 1914 AND AFTERWARDS

1. Médéric Martin was elected mayor of Montreal in 1914, 1916, 1918, and 1921. He was defeated in 1924, but was re-elected in 1926. In 1928, he was defeated by Camillien Houde and did not stand for election again.

2. On the occasion of Martin's death in June 1946, the press carried many appreciations. Those of *La Presse* and *La Patrie* were the fullest.

3. ROBERT RUMILLY, *Histoire de la Province de Québec* (Montréal: Valiquette, nd.), vol. XIII, *Henri Bourassa*, p. 183.

4. *Le Devoir*, 11 a 14 mars 1914.

5. The vote by polling-place was recorded in some newspapers, *e.g. The Gazette* and *Star*.

6. *The Gazette*, March 10, 1914.

7. G. W. L. NICHOLSON, *The Canadian Expeditionary Force* (Ottawa: the Queen's Printer, 1964), chap. 2, "Forging the Weapon."

8. There is no First Great War history of either Montreal university. Some notion of the variety of military service rendered may be obtained from *McGill's Honour Roll* (Montreal: privately printed, 1926).

9. J. MURRAY GIBBON, *The Steel of Empire* (Indianapolis: Bobbs Merrill, 1935), chap. 31, The CPR and the War."

10. J. D. SCOTT, *Vickers, a History* (London: Weidenfeld and Nicolson, 1962), and

GADDIS SMITH, *Britain's Clandestine Submarines* (New Haven: Yale University Press, 1964); also information supplied by the Canadian Vickers Company.

CHAPTER 16: PROSPERITY—DEPRESSION—WAR

1. W. B. HOWELL,
Francis John Shepherd, Surgeon
(Toronto: J. M. Dent, 1934),
p. 221.

2. LUCIEN FAVREAU and
ROGER CHARBONNEAU,
"La Finance", *Montréal
Economique*, ed. Esdras Minville
(Montréal: Editions Fides, 1943).
Pp. 282-99 provide a valuable
statement on banks and banking.

3. H. A. INNIS,
"The Rise and Decline of
Toronto," *Canadian Forum*, vol.
XIII (April 1933), no. 157. The
newspaper referred to was the
Globe.

4. L. C. TOMBS,
The Port of Montreal (Toronto:
Macmillan Company, 1928),
p. 40; also,

M. LAFORET,
"Evolution du port de Montréal"
(unpublished thesis, Ecole des
Hautes Etudes commerciales,
1942).

5. J. D. SCOTT,
Vickers, a History (London:
Weidenfeld and Nicolson, 1962),
p. 167.

6. Information supplied by the
British American Oil Company;
the Imperial Oil Company of
Canada; Texaco Canada Limited;
also,

YVAN VERSAILLES,
"Le developpement industriel de
Montréal" (Ecole des Hautes
Etudes commerciales thesis,
1938).

7. G. W. STEPHENS
manuscript collection, Redpath
Library, McGill University.
Included are notes and drafts for
Stephens's *The St. Lawrence
Waterway* (Montreal, 1930).

8. F. H. ELLIS, *Canada's Flying
Heritage* (Toronto: University of
Toronto Press, 1954), p. 273.

9. CHARLES RENAUD, *L'imprévisible Monsieur Houde* (Montréal:
Les Editions de l'Homme, 1964), an
admirable appreciation of Houde
by his secretary.

10. The Montreal press gave full
coverage to the election. It was
generally favourable to Houde.

11. P. LAPORTE,
*Le vrai visage de Maurice
Duplessis* (Montréal: Les
Editions de l'Homme, 1960).
The English edition, *The True Face
of Maurice Duplessis*, contains
valuable additional biographical
information.

12. RENAUD,
L'imprévisible Monsieur Houde,
p. 26.

13. J. I. COOPER,
The Blessed Communion
(Montreal: Diocese of Montreal,
1960), p.184.

14. The address was delivered on
October 25, 1935. It was printed
in pamphlet form.

15. C. BETRAND,
Histoire de Montréal (2 vols.;
Montréal: Beauchemin, 1935 and
1942), vol. II, chap. 8; also,

HONORE PARENT,
"L'administration municipale,"
Montreal Economique, ed.
Esdras Minville (Montréal:
Editions Fides, 1943), chap. 8.

16. Montreal press, October 1936;
also, "Quebec's Fascists Show
their Hand," *Canadian Forum*
(December 1936), vol. XVI,
no. 191.

CHAPTER 17: THE GREAT TRANSFORMATION

1. BENOIT BROUILLETTE,
"Le port de Montréal,"
L'Actualité Economique, vol. II
(no. 2, 1935).

2. J. A. RETTY,
"Iron Ore Galore," *Canadian
Geographical Journal*, vol. XLII
(no. 1, January, 1951).

3. W. S. WHITE,
Pages from the History of Sorel
(Berthierville, P.Q.: Quebec Iron
Ore and Titanium Corp., 1958);
also,

M. H. SINCLAIR,
"The Industrial Geography of the
Beauharnois Canal Area"
(McGill University thesis, 1954).

6. BENOIT BROUILLETTE,
"Le Port et les Transports," and

JEAN DELAGE,
"L'Industrie manufacturière,
Montréal Economique ed. Esdras
Minville (Montréal: Editions Fides,
1943), chaps. 4 and 5.

5. REX DESMARCHAIS, "La
Commission des Ecoles
Catholiques de Montréal en 1946,"
L'Ecole Canadienne (Montréal:
Commission des Ecoles catholiques,
1942), pp. 31-49.

4. Information supplied by the
schools mentioned. There is no
study of the independent school
in Montreal, nor of any school.

7. H. C. CROSS,
*One Hundred Years of Service
with Youth, the Story of the
Montreal YMCA* (Montreal:
YMCA Central Board, 1951),
p. 354.

8. C. BERTRAND,
Histoire de Montréal (2 vols.;
Montréal: Beauchemin, 1935 and
1942). Vol. II has a brief but
valuable note, pp. 257-59, on the
later archbishops.

9. *L'inauguration des nouveaux
immeubles de l'Université de
Montréal de Mont-Royal le 3 juin
1943* (Montréal, 1943).

10. Speculation concerning
Archbishop Charbonneau's
resignation is reflected in
contemporary writing: *Rélations*,
Xème année, no. 111 (mars 1950),
and *Cité libre*, XIème année,

no. 124 (janvier-février 1960).
Interesting sidelights on archbishops Gauthier and Charbonneau
(entirely unconnected with the
latter's resignation) are contained in

M. G. BALLANTYNE,
"The Catholic Church and the
CCF," *Canadian Catholic
Historical Association Annual
Report 1963*, pp. 33-45. A highly
sympathetic appreciation of
Archbishop Charbonneau is
provided by Renaude Laporte,
*L'Histoire bouleversante de Mgr
Charbonneau* (Montréal: Les
Editions du Jour, 1962).

11. The Ninth Census of Canada
(1931) placed the largest number
of employed Montrealers (over
71,000) in service occupations.
About one-fifth were professional
persons, the remainder were in
jobs that required very little skill.
In addition, there were over fifty
thousand unskilled labourers.

12. *Jean Drapeau vous parle*
(Montréal: Editions de la Cité,
1959), Preface by André
Laurendeau.

13. ANTHONY CLEGG,
The Mount Royal Tunnel
(Canadian Railway Historical
Society, Montreal, 1963).

14. Information supplied by
Dupuis Frères, T. Eaton Company,
Henry Morgan's, and Holt
Renfrew & Company.

15. LESLIE ROBERTS,
Maclean's Magazine (April 18,
1964), vol. LXXVII, no. 7.

16. RAYMOND GRENIER,
Regards sur l'Expo 67 (2 vols.;
Montréal: Les Editions de l'Homme,
1965), vol. I.

17. HENRY MOTT
manuscript collection, McGill
University.

18. HAROLD KAPLAN,
The Regional City (Toronto:
CBC, 1965). There is no modern
full-scale study of Canadian city
government. The chapter
"Metropolitan Government" in
Professor Kaplan's admirable
lecture series goes far to repair
this deficiency.

A NOTE
REGARDING
SOURCES

BOOKS
1. Special studies are listed in the notes on each chapter.

2. General histories of Montreal: W. H. Atherton, *History of Montreal,* 1535-1914 (3 vols.; Montreal: S. J. Clarke Publishing Company, 1914); Camille Bertrand, *Histoire de Montréal* (2 vols.; Montréal: Beauchemin, 1935 and 1942); J. I. Cooper, *Montreal, the Story of Three Hundred Years* (Montreal: L'Imprimerie Lamirande, 1942); Kathleen Jenkins, *Montreal, Island City of the St. Lawrence* (Garden City: Doubleday & Company, Inc., 1966); Stephen Leacock, *Montreal, Seaport and City* (Garden City: Doubleday Doran, 1943). Indispensable for placing Montreal in its physical and historical setting are: Raoul Blanchard, *Montréal, équisse de géographie urbaine* (Grenoble: Etudes canadiennes, 1947), and Robert Rumilly, *Histoire de la Province de Quebéc* (31 vols.; Bernard Valiquette, Montréal, 1940-59).

MANUSCRIPTS AND THEIR WHEREABOUTS
The civic and judicial records of Montreal are kept in the Archives of the City of Montreal (City Hall) and in the Montreal Judicial District Archives (Old Court House). The earliest registers of civil status are in the possession of the *fabrique* of Notre Dame Church.

More general manuscript collections. consisting of letters, diaries, and business correspondence, are held by the Bibliothèque de Saint-Sulpice, the Chateau de Ramezay, McGill University, the Montreal Municipal Library, St. Mary's College, and the Université de Montréal. The best general sources for business history of the nineteenth and twentieth centuries are the minutes and registers of correspondence of the Chambre de Commerce de Montréal (1887), the Montreal Board of Trade (1822), and the National Harbours Commission.

Outside Montreal, the Public Archives of Canada (Ottawa) and the Archives de la Province de Québec have important manuscript collections bearing on Montreal.

NEWSPAPERS
The Canadian Library Association, Ottawa, has microfilmed the major Montreal newspapers. Files of the

newspapers themselves are held by a number of Montreal libraries. The holdings of the Bibliothèque de Saint-Sulpice, the Fraser-Hickson Institute, and the Montreal Municipal Library are particularly notable. Outside Montreal, the most extensive newspaper collection is that of the Library of Parliament (Ottawa).

NON-LITERARY SOURCES

The most extensive collection of pictorial material in various media is in the Archives of the City of Montreal. The Archives also possesses a map collection. Other notable collections of pictures are those of the Chateau de Ramezay and of McGill University. The latter has the photographs of William Notman.

There are two published collections of Montreal pictures: *Montreal, a Pictorial Record,* compiled by Volpi and Winkworth (Montreal, 1963); and Gustave Lanctôt, "Images et figures de Montréal sous la France, 1642-1763," *Transactions and Proceedings of the Royal Society of Canada* (1943). The latter is a work of great erudition and is of the highest historical value.

Acknowledgement has been made of the importance of the *Canadian Illustrated News, Dominion Illustrated, Illustrated London News,* and *Opinion Publique* for illustrations of late nineteenth century Montreal. There is no comparable record for the later period. The weekend editions of *La Presse* and of the *Montreal Standard* should not be neglected.

STATISTICS

The various administrative departments of the City of Montreal, finance, planning, welfare, etc. issue valuable statistical statements. The decennial censuses of Canada (1851-1961) provide information on population, occupation, employment, etc. The Canadian censuses make it possible to study Montreal in relation to other cities. The *Annuaire statistique de la Province de Québec* (1917-62) contains valuable digests of information on Montreal.

INDEX

A

Abbott, Sir John; *see* Mayors
Academie Mont Saint-Louis, 131
Accommodation, 12
Act of Union, (1840), 38
Act Respecting Communist Propaganda (Padlock Law), 170
Air Canada (Trans-Canada Airlines), 160
Air Meets, 122-23
Aitken, Max (Lord Beaverbrook), 115-18
Allan, Sir Hugh, 17, 46, 48, 49
Allan Line (Montreal Ocean Steamship Company), 17, 73, 156
American Revolution, 5, 8
Ames, Herbert Brown, 90, 93
Ames-Holden Company, 89, 90, 114
Angus, R. B., 54
Angus Shops, 113, 126, 148
Annexations, 99-101, 127
Anti-Semitism, 170
Arnold, Matthew, 70
Art Association of Montreal, 67
Asselin, J. O. 186
Associés de Notre-Dame (Associates of Notre Dame), 2-3, 24
Atholstan, Lord; *see* Graham, Hugh
Atwater Aqueduct, 27
Automobile, 106
Auto-routes, 176

B

Baldwin, Robert, 43
Ballantyne, C. C., 142
Banking, location of in late nineteenth century, 74
Banks: Bank of Montreal: 10, 25, 38, 56, 74, 114, 115, 116; Bank of Upper Canada, 45; Banque Canadienne Nationale, 152; Banque Provinciale Nationale, 152; Canada Banking Company, 10; Canadian Imperial Bank of Commerce, 189; Commercial Bank, 45; Merchants' Bank of Halifax, 114; Royal Bank of Canada, 114, 152
Baron de Hirsch Institute, 94
Bassett, John, 118
Beauharnois: Canals, 11, 175; Power Corporation, 155, 157-58
Beatty, Sir Edward, 167
Beaugrand, Honoré; *see* Mayors
Beaver Hall Hill, 5, 31, 74
Beaver Line, 46
Beaverbrook, Lord; *see* Max Aitken
Bell Telephone Company, 108, 114, 125, 153
Berthiaume, Trefflé, 117
Berri Street (east wall), 20, 75
Bertram, Alexander, 97
Bethune, Rev. John, 8
Birks, Henry and Company, 74, 125
Black Watch, 146, 173
Bloc populaire, 186
Bonaventure Hall, 37
Bonaventure Station, 55
Bonaventure Street, 103

Bond, Rev. W.B., later Archbishop of Montreal, 32
Bonsecours Market House, 15, 73
Booth, John Wilkes, 34
Booth, General William, 89
Bordeaux Prison, 114
Boucherville, 37
Boundaries of Montreal: late nineteenth century, 74; early, 20 *see also* Berri and McGill Streets
Bourassa, Henri, 120, 131, 134, 139, 145, 159
Bourgeoys, Marguerite, 3
Bourget, Bishop Ignace, 20, 22, 61, 66, 75, 82, 83
Bout de l'Ile, 173, 106
Bovey, Professor John, 110
Bradley, Dr. George, 106
Bread Riot, 82
Bridges: Champlain, 176; Jacques Cartier, 50, 155, 176; Lachine (CPR), 55, 128, 129, 176; Mercier, 176; Royal Albert, 50; Sir Louis LaFontaine, 176; Victoria, 14, 73, 155, 176
British and Canadian School Association, 64
British North America Act, 43
Brothers of the Christian Schools, 64, 162
Brown, George, 41
Bruchési, Canon Paul, later Archbishop of Montreal, 95, 124, 181
Brymner, Douglas, 67
Bureau des Pauvres, 4
Butler, Samuel, 59, 71

C

Canadian Broadcasting Corporation, 169
Canadian Century, 116
Canadian College, Rome, 182
Canadian Illustrated News, 108
Canadian Pacific Steamships, 57-58, 156
Canadian Press, 119-20
Canadian Rubber Company, 140
Canadian Vickers Company, 149
Cannon Commission, 132-33
Capitulation of Montreal (1760), 5-6
Carnivals, winter, 80
Caron, Mr. Justice François, 185
Carter, Edward, 42
Cartier, Sir George-Etienne, 22, 31, 39-43, 46, 48, 49, 158
Cartier, Jacques, 1, 2, 175
Cathedral: Anglican, 30, 31; Roman Catholic, 20, 22, 23, 56, 74, 75
Catholic Sailors' Club, 156
Cattle export, 112
Caughnawaga, 4
Cemeteries; 30, 65, 76, 82, 83, 158
Central Station, 188
Cession of Canada, 4-7, 9
Chamberlain, Brown, 32, 69
Chambre de Commerce du District de Montréal, 77, 133
Champs de Mars, 109, 145
Champagne Commission, 192
Champlain, Samuel de, 1, 2
Chapleau, Sir Adolphe, 87, 88
Charbonneau, Archbishop Joseph, 181, 182

S

T

U

V

W

Y